The
BATH TRAMWAYS

by
Colin G. Maggs

THE OAKWOOD PRESS

© C.G. Maggs and The OAKWOOD PRESS 1992

ISBN 0 85361 392 3

First published 1971

Second Revised Edition 1992

Typeset by Gem Publishing Company, Brightwell, Wallingford, Oxfordshire.

Printed and bound by Alphaprint, Witney, Oxfordshire.

Acknowledgements

Unfortunately the company's minute books were not available and sources have been mainly contemporary newspaper and magazine accounts supplemented by memories of employees. The author is greatly indebted to the latter, too numerous to mention individually, who have helped him enormously. Thanks are also due to the Bristol Omnibus Company; R. Bryant, Bath Record Office; I.P. Collis, Somerset Record Office; the Keeper, Public Record Office and the staff of Bath Reference Library. Especial thanks must be given to Dr J.L. Batten; S.A. Gardener; and W. Gingell and J.C. Gillham who checked the manuscript, the latter also providing maps and additional information.

Books used were: *The Story of G.F. Milnes*, (J.H. Price); *Tramways of the West of England*, (P.W. Gentry); Minute Books of Bath City Council and sub-committees. Newspapers and magazines consulted were: *Bath Argus*; *Bath & Cheltenham Gazette*; *Bath Chronicle*; *Bath Herald*; *Bath Journal*; *Bath & County Graphic*; *Bladud*; B.E.T. timetables and rule book; *Commercial Motor*; *Electrician*; *Electrical Engineer*; *Electrical Investments*; *Electrical Review*; *Electrical Times*; *Engineering*; *Keene's Bath Journal*; *Light Railway & Tramway World*; *Tramway & Railway World*, the deposited plans of various schemes, the 1880 Act of Parliament, and six subsequent Light Railway Orders.

Title page: Rear of tramcar 26 in Kingsmead Square *en route* to Weston c.1909. In the early years, two advertisements were usually carried at the ends, whereas in later years the advert ran completely across the front giving a much neater appearance.

Author's Collection

Published by
The OAKWOOD PRESS
P.O.Box 122, Headington, Oxford.

Contents

	Acknowledgements	2
Chapter One	Horse Tramways	5
Chapter Two	Electric Cars Begin	17
Chapter Three	From 1910 onwards	35
Chapter Four	Rolling Stock	49
Chapter Five	The Permanent Way and Electrical Equipment	61
Chapter Six	Operation	69
Chapter Seven	Accidents	101

Public road transport in pre-tramway days – a coach arriving at the Saracen's Head, Broad Street.   *Author's Collection*

Horse tram ticket.

Public transport in the pre-Bath Tramways era: a 2-ton steam carriage on the Bath to London road in 1829. Built by Sir Goldsworthy Gurney it was fired by a mixture of coke and charcoal placed on the lower arms of U-shaped water tubes forming the boiler. Cylinders and water tank were underslung to keep down the centre of gravity.

Oakwood Collection

Chapter One

Horse Tramways

The City of Bath, with its narrow streets and steep hills, was unsuitable for a large-scale horse tramway system, but in September 1878 two short lines were proposed: Lambridge to the top of Broad Street, and one linking the Great Western and Midland stations. The following year more ambitious propositions were made, including routes to Combe Down, Lansdown and Weston, and a Batheaston—Twerton scheme with a rail-less section in Milsom Street. The exact rail-less system to be adopted is not known.

In November 1879 the Bath Corporation accepted a proposition by the Bristol Tramways Co. Ltd, which had been formed in July 1874, for a line in Bath from Grosvenor to the GWR station, via Pierrepont Street, but front-agers objected, and so the route was altered in February 1880 to run via Southgate Street. Bath Corporation demanded a deposit of £1500 security, as it was afraid the company might tear up the streets, go bankrupt and be unable to re-instate them. This sum was in addition to the £1000 deposit in the Court of Chancery required by the Tramways Act of 1870.

In July 1880 Bath Tramways Co. Ltd was formed, with a capital of £50,000 in £10 shares subscribed by Bristolians. The Chairman was William Butler, Secretary George White, and Henry Gale Gardener, Charles Hoskins Low and Thomas Davey as Directors. The surveyor and assistant surveyor were Parfitt and Fortune. For many years George White was also the Managing Director, and William Butler the Chairman, of the Bristol Tramways Co. Ltd. Four of the eight Bath promoters were also Bristol Directors.

At the end of 1879 application was made by the Bristol promoters for a Bath Tramways Order under the Tramways Act of 1870. This was duly granted, but it had no legal force until it was confirmed by Parliament by the Tramways Orders Confirmation (No. 1) Act, of 1880, which received the Royal Assent on 26th August, 1880, as 43 & 44 Vic.cap. clxxii (172). This Act sanctioned no fewer than 17 different tramway schemes, which was considerably more than almost all other Confirmation Acts either before or after, the 17 being for tramways in Bath, Birkdale, Bristol, Cambridge, Cardiff, Croydon, Darlington, Dudley, Ipswich, Llanelly, Merthyr, Peterborough, Staffordshire, Stockton-on-Tees, Sunderland, Withington, and Wolverhampton.

This Bath Tramways Order of 1880 authorised the newly-formed Bath Tramways Co. Ltd to purchase and acquire such lands as they might require, or to sell or dispose of such lands, provided that they must not at any time hold more than five acres of land. The Promoters were also authorised to construct, and for at least 21 years to maintain, the following tramways, with all proper rails, points, junctions, plates, offices, weigh-bridges, stables, carriage-houses, warehouses, works, and conveniences connected therewith, and to work and use the same.

Tramway No. 1, wholly in the parish of Twerton, was to commence in Lower Bristol Road opposite the passenger entrance to Twerton GWR station, then pass along the Lower Bristol Road as far as the Midland Arms public house. It was to be all single line, except double line from the start for a length of two chains and from

Staff of the Bath Tramways Company outside the depot at the Porter Butt Hotel on 5th
September, 1881.   *Author's Collection*

Twelve-seat horse tram No. 1 waits at the Grosvenor terminus *c.*1898 prior to starting
for the GWR station. The garter surrounding the figure 1 bears the inscription 'Road
Car and Tramways Co'.   *Author's Collection*

the Royal Oak public house for three chains westward. The total length was 58.28 chains, of which 53.28 chains were single line and five chains double line.

Tramway No. 2, beginning in the parish of Twerton opposite the Midland Arms, was to pass along Lower Bristol Road, across the Old Bridge, and along Dorchester Street, to terminate in the roadway opposite Bath GWR station at a point in the parish of St James 1½ chains eastward from the cabman's shelter. This was to be all single line, except double from the start for a length of three chains, from 1½ chains west to 1½ chains east of Green Park Tavern, from the corner of Wells Road to a point three chains west, and for the last two chains before the terminus. The total length was 72.90 chains, of which 61.90 chains were single line and 11 chains double line.

Tramway No. 4 was to start in High Street opposite the entrance to the Guildhall and pass along High Street, Northgate Street, Walcot Street, Ladymead, Cornwell Buildings, London Street, and London Road, to terminate in London Road at a point in the parish of Swainswick opposite the east side of Gloucester Road. This was to be all single line, except it was double from a point one chain south of St Michael's Church to a point in Ladymead opposite the steps leading to the Paragon; from a point one chain north of the southern side of the Penitentiary Chapel in Cornwell Buildings to a point three chains northward therefrom; from a point one chain west of the lamp-post at the junction of Cleveland Place and London Street for a length of three chains eastward; from Piccadilly Place for a length of three chains eastward; and from a point opposite the east end of Beaufort Buildings West for a length of three chains eastward. In Walcot Street the tramway was to be laid so that the centre of each line was one foot from the centre line of the street, and only one of such lines was to be used at one and the same time. (This of course was the legal language describing what is normally known as interlaced track.) The total length of Tramway No. 4 was 1 mile 36.48 chains, of which 1 mile 9.10 chains were single line and 27.38 chains double line.

Tramway No. 5 was to continue from the end of No. 4, further along London Road, to end in the parish of Batheaston five chains north-east of the entrance into Batheaston Lodge. This was to be wholly single line, for a total length of 67.90 chains.

Tramway No. 6 was to commence in the parish of St James, in Southgate Street, opposite the north side of Broad Quay, passing thence along Southgate Street, Stall Street, Cheap Street, and High Street, to end in High Street in the parish of St Peter and St Paul, at a point one chain south of the entrance of the Guildhall. This was to be all single line, except double from 1½ chains south to 1½ chains north of St James' Church, and from one chain west of the east end of Cheap Street to the end of this tramway. The total length was 28.70 chains, of which 22.70 chains were single line and six chains double line.

The total length of route authorised was thus 4 miles 24.26 chains, of which 3 miles 54.88 chains were single line and 49.38 chains double. Tramway No. 3 was deleted from the application, and did not appear in the Order but it was intended to be from Bath GWR station, along Manvers Street, Pierrepoint Street, Terrace Walks, and Orange Grove, to the Guildhall in High Street, i.e. from the end of No. 2 to the start of No. 4. This also would account for the missing gap of one chain between the end of No. 6 and the start of No. 4 as described in the Order. No. 6 was an addition in March 1880 subsequent to the original application and in substitution for No. 3.

The Order, and therefore also the Confirmation Act, said the tramways shall be constructed on a gauge of four feet, and no carriage used on the tramways shall exceed six feet in width. On roads which already were paved with wood the Promoters had to pave the road between the tramway rails, and for 18 inches on

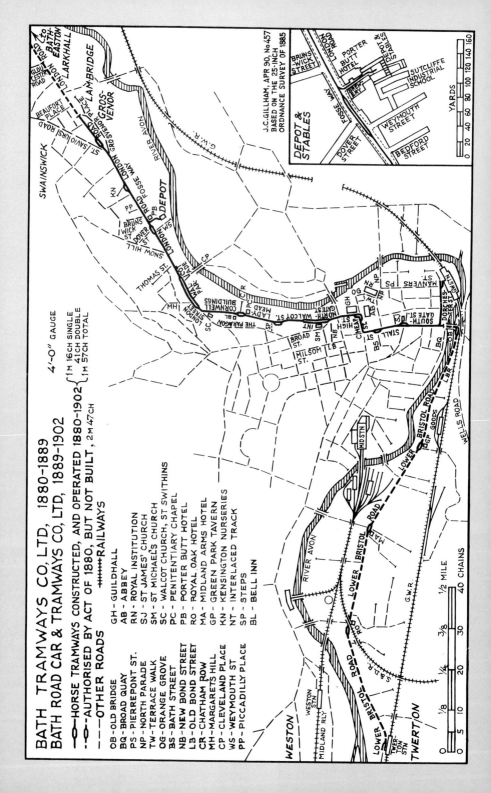

BATH TRAMWAYS CO., LTD., 1880–1889
BATH ROAD CAR & TRAMWAYS CO., LTD, 1889–1902

4'-0" GAUGE

—— HORSE TRAMWAYS CONSTRUCTED, AND OPERATED 1880-1902 { 1M 16CH SINGLE / 41CH DOUBLE
—·—·— AUTHORISED BY ACT OF 1880, BUT NOT BUILT, 2M 47CH 1M 57CH TOTAL
— — — OTHER ROADS
++++++ RAILWAYS

OB – OLD BRIDGE
BQ – BROAD QUAY
PS – PIERREPONT ST.
NP – NORTH PARADE
TW – TERRACE WALK
OG – ORANGE GROVE
BS – BATH STREET
NB – NEW BOND STREET
LB – OLD BOND STREET
CR – CHATHAM ROW
MH – MARGARET'S HILL
CP – CLEVELAND PLACE
WS – WEYMOUTH ST
PP – PICCADILLY PLACE

GH – GUILDHALL
AB – ABBEY
RN – ROYAL INSTITUTION
SJ – ST JAMES' CHURCH
SM – ST MICHAEL'S CHURCH
SC – WALCOT CHURCH, ST SWITHINS
PC – PENITENTIARY CHAPEL
PB – PORTER BUTT HOTEL
RO – ROYAL OAK HOTEL
MA – MIDLAND ARMS HOTEL
GP – GREEN PARK TAVERN
KN – KENSINGTON NURSERIES
NT – INTERLACED TRACK
SP – STEPS
BL – BELL INN

J.C.GILLHAM, APR 90, No.A57
BASED ON THE 25-INCH
ORDNANCE SURVEY OF 1885

each side, with wood, and to keep the same so paved. The rails were to be such as the Board of Trade may approve, and the Board could from time to time require the Promoters to adopt and apply such improvements in the tramways and the rails as experience might from time to time suggest. If the Promoters did not keep the tramway in good condition and repair, so as not to be a danger or annoyance to the ordinary traffic, they were to pay a penalty not exceeding five pounds for every day on which such default continued. They were authorised to make all such additional crossings, passing places, sidings, junctions, and other works, as might from time to time be necessary, or for providing access to any stables, carriage houses, sheds or works, subject to the approval of the road authority.

The Order allowed the tramways to be used for conveying passengers, animals, goods, minerals, and parcels, but the Promoters were not bound to carry such items unless they thought fit, other than passengers' luggage up to 28 lb. in weight. If any animals, goods, minerals, or parcels were carried they were to be in separate carriages, or separate parts of carriages set apart for that purpose. No passenger cars were to be run before 2 pm on any Sunday, Good Friday, or Christmas Day, and cars must not be run on any of those days past any church or place of worship during the hours of divine service beyond a walking pace, unless a penalty of 40 shillings for each offence was paid. Ordinary fares were fixed at 2d. maximum, but the Promoters were obliged to run Workmen's cars every weekday not later than 7 am and not earlier than 6 pm for artisans, mechanics, and daily labourers at not more than ½d. per mile, with a one penny minimum.

A very detailed list of maximum tolls and charges can be summarised as 6d. per mile for large animals and 3d. for small ones; 3d. per mile per ton for coals, chalk, sand, cinders, manure and road materials, etc; 4d. per mile per ton for iron, bricks, stone, tiles, and clay, etc; 6d. per mile per ton for sugar, corn, flour, timber, nails, chains, cotton, wool, drugs, and fish, etc; 3d., 5d., 7d. or 9d. for any distance for parcels according to weight; and 2s. per mile for single articles of great weight exceeding four tons. As security to Bath Corporation for the due completion to their reasonable satisfaction of the tramways, the Promoters were required within two months after the passing of this Act to deposit £1500 with the Corporation, this sum to be held for three years, and 4 per cent per annum interest to be paid on it.

Augustus Krauss of Colston Street, Bristol, won the contract for laying the permanent way, and by 22nd September, 1880 was working in Walcot Street, the City Surveyor barring traffic from Walcot Street for seven days from 27th September to expedite the laying. Stall Street, Cheap Street and High Street were also closed for various periods for track-laying, causing inconvenience, and so aggrieving shopkeepers that they posted up notices and employed sandwich-board men with placards 'Tenders wanted for the Immediate Removal of the Blockade and the Rubbish. Apply to the Neighbouring Tradesmen'. In the dark, people stumbled over the rails awaiting laying.

In December, Matthew Hill was appointed manager of Bath Tramways (he had been an inspector on Bristol Tramways), and on 10th December George White wrote to the Board of Trade from the joint Bristol and Bath Tramway Company's offices at 31, Clare Street, Bristol, to inform them that everything was ready for inspection. This was carried out on 23rd December by Major General Hutchinson.

The tramway was formally opened by the Mayor on 24th December when most of the members of the Corporation rode from the GWR station to

Horse Car No. 4 in Southgate Street *en route* to the GWR station.   *Author's Collection*

A Bath Electric Tramways parcel delivery van in Laura Place *c.*1908.   *Lens of Sutton*

Grosvenor, and on returning were entertained to luncheon at the Grand Pump Room Hotel. The cars were pulled by two horses on this occasion, but one horse was used normally.

The route thus opened comprised a small part of Tramway No. 2 in the 1880 Order, the whole of No. 6, and most of No. 4, making a total route length of only 1 mile 57 chains, of which 1 mile 16 chains were single line and 41 chains were double. All the passing loops on Tramways Nos. 6 and 4 as specified in the Act were so constructed, except the one at Piccadilly Place, and three additional three-chain loops were also provided right from the start: in Stall Street opposite the end of Bath Street; in London Road opposite the end of Dover Street; and in London Road opposite the Kensington Nurseries. The Cleveland Place loop was made substantially larger than the normal 3 chains as specified in the Act, and it commenced just south of Margaret's Hill, but instead of Walcot Street being double for 15.38 chains throughout it was built as single with a loop at each end and a length of interlaced track northward from the southern loop. No subsequent extensions were ever made, and tramways Nos. 1, 3, 5, most of 2, and the outer end of 4 were never constructed, and their powers lapsed in 1884.

The car depot and stables were south of London Road, just beyond the eastern end of the Dover Street passing loop, hidden behind the Porter Butt Hotel and Kensington Brewery, access being by a narrow alleyway between these two, the depot abutting onto the side of the Sutcliffe Industrial School buildings. All these structures remained unchanged throughout the whole life of the horse tramways from 1880 to 1904 and indeed until the 1970s, the Porter Butt Hotel (only) being still unaltered in 1992.

In February 1881, as all the company's capital had been spent, George White asked for the £1500 security to be returned and the Council complied. White said that work on the extension to Twerton would begin as soon as the first dividend had been declared.

At the first half-yearly meeting a dividend of 6 per cent was declared, despite difficulties caused by snow in the first three months, and 237,041 passengers were carried in the first seven months. The next meeting's report was not so pleasant — owing to dullness of trade and fine weather encouraging people to walk, only 170,863 passengers were carried, and the dividend fell to 4 per cent. The trams were nearly empty between the station and New Bond Street, and it was hoped that a 1d. fare for this stage would fill them. To increase receipts further, the manager introduced a parcel service. The Directors said they could not see their way to raising capital for the extension to Twerton. In April 1882, Hill moved to Wolverhampton and Randolph W. Roan, who had been in sole charge of the Horfield line, Bristol, took over the managership.

By September 1882, receipts had fallen so much that the small profits would not allow any dividend — this was blamed on the wet weather which had put excursionists off visiting the city. The fare reduction from the station to New Bond Street increased receipts, and in March 1883 the company was just earning enough to pay interest on the debentures. Both Secretary and Directors accepted a reduced remuneration that year, saving £100. To make matters worse, the horses had been struck by an epidemic of pink-eye. The number of passengers carried in the first half of 1883 was 156,000 and in the second half, 159,858 — considerably short of the first year's working.

On 11th March, 1884, the city council met White, who proposed a lease of the line for 21 years at a rental not exceeding £210 per annum, on condition that the Corporation bought the rolling stock and horses. Negotiations fell through, and new ones opened with the Patent Cable Tramways Corporation, the cable system being thought very suitable for Bath hills. They offered £7,500 payable partly in cash and partly in new debentures. As the current mortgage debentures, interest and debts amounted to nearly the purchase money, the Directors hoped the creditors would waive a percentage of their claims so that the Directors could secure £1,200 for division among shareholders.

At an extraordinary meeting held on 8th May, 1884, shareholders unanimously agreed to the sale, and the Deed of Transfer was signed on 26th May. The Cable Co. had £130,000 capital and spent £1,000 on improvements to Bath tramways, and bought seven lightweight 12 seater cars (for horse traction: cable was not used by the company in spite of its name). However, J. McCarnen, the Cable Co's manager, was no more successful at running the system than Bath Tramways Co., and in 1888 the company was in liquidation. All the assets of the Patent Cable Tramways Co. were sold to Dick, Kerr & Co. Ltd, of London and Kilmarnock, on 11th August, 1888.

The Bath Omnibus Road Car Co. Ltd, formed in 1886, took possession of the tramway from Dick, Kerr & Co. Ltd on 31st December, 1888, and purchased it for £5,500 on 1st April, 1889, on which date it also changed its own name to the Bath Road Car & Tramways Co. Ltd. To meet the cost of purchase, it invited subscription for £4,000 in £1 shares and 40 debenture bonds of £50. This was a prudent move as the Road Car Co. already ran buses, and with the tramway system, it now had practically a monopoly of traffic. The BRCT offices were at 8 Old Bond Street, Bath.

The original company had been formed with a capital of £4,000 for purchasing and carrying on the omnibus and road car business of Henry Gould to Weston and Twerton, and that of Frederick Lavington to Batheaston and Bathford. Its Chairman was Major James Wedgwood Yeeles; Managing Director Henry Gould, with Solomon Francis, George Weaver, H.W. Bowles Directors, George Hext Secretary, and Traffic Manager Arthur Edwin White. When the tramway system was bought, W. Lewis joined the Board. The company was flourishing enough to pay 10 per cent dividend. They took over from Dick, Kerr 25 horses and harness, 7 cars, 90 tons of unlaid steel rails, stables, and the right to receive back the amount deposited with the Board of Trade. The net profit of the last two years of Cable Co. operation was £744 19s. 5d., and if this continued, it would have given the Road Car Co. nearly 7 per cent of the purchase money. The permanent way had been in such a poor state that one man was fatally injured by the rails being two inches above the road, and cart and carriage axles were broken.

At the first annual meeting of the Bath Road Car Co. on 7th August, 1889, it was announced that in the three months of tramway operation, it had increased receipts compared with the old company and out of the total of

697,209 passengers carried by the buses for twelve months and trams for three months, 324,062 had been carried by the trams. The permanent way had been put into a good state and the tramcars renovated. A dividend of 7½ per cent was declared.

In the exceptionally long winter of 1891, blizzards caused expenses of £500 for snow removal, and trams and buses were stopped for days on end. (On 14th February, 1888, 1 ft. of snow had stopped trams for a day, but they ran on the following day with two horses drawing them.) A contract was signed with the Post Office to carry their servants for £50, though this was abandoned the following year when it was discovered that the ordinary tariff for the postmen would have brought in £300–£400 per annum. The Road Car Co. asked the Post Office for £150, later reducing it to £120, but they would not go over £100.

In subsequent years the company paid a dividend of 5 to 7 per cent, and in January, 1896, the 40 £50 debentures became payable; 26 were renewed, the remaining 14 being bought by the Directors for the reserve fund, so that it then paid 4½ per cent instead of the 3 per cent they received from Government securities.

Tram receipts in 1897 were slightly less than the previous year, and some suggested that on the expiration of the tramway's 21-year lease, the rails should be lifted, but W. Lewis, who had become Chairman on the death of Yeeles on 10th March, 1893, thought this unwise as the trams rendered a great public service and contributed to the rates. The following year showed a fall of £130 in tram receipts, and a further drop of £30 in 1898 through the opposition of their own buses — the bus fare from the eastern end of Larkhall to Old Bond Street was 1d., whereas the tram fare for the shorter distance Grosvenor–Abbey was 2d.

R.H. Moore became Chairman in 1900 on the death of Lewis. The company prospered, paying an average dividend of 7½ per cent over 12 years, and at the annual meeting on 15th August, 1900, an extraordinary meeting was held to consider the advisability of increasing the share capital of the company from £10,000 to £15,000 by the creation of 5,000 new ordinary shares. On 19th September it was decided that 3,000 of the shares be offered at par to existing shareholders in proportion to the number of shares held by them; the rest to be issued by the Directors at a premium. Henry Gould still remained the Managing Director.

After a dispute over price and subsequent arbitration by Sir Frederick Bramwell, in 1902 the tramway was purchased for £5,210 by the Corporation on behalf of the promoters of the Bath Electric Tramways. The latter obtained £446 13s. 3d. from the sale of cars, horses and office equipment, and on 25th July the last horse tram ran, Councillor Tuckett riding on the last car as he did on the first. The following day a supplementary service of horse buses commenced running from Larkhall to the GWR station avoiding Walcot Street and proceeding via the Paragon and Milsom Street. On 27th August, 1902 the company altered its name to the Bath Carriage & Omnibus Ltd and continued running buses until 19th February, 1904, when competition from electric trams put it out of business, causing suffering to parts of the city not served by electric cars.

Staff

The drivers and conductors had a hard life, working from 8 am to 11 pm and 2–10 pm on Sundays, making a 98-hour week. The drivers were paid 24s. a week, later reduced to 18s., but were only entitled to a day's notice of dismissal, whereas they had to give the company seven days' notice of intention to leave. Conductors wore high crown caps and had a leather satchel over their shoulder for money. They had to go before the Chief Constable to be approved and the proprietor paid 2s. 6d. for a conductor's licence. Conductors wore a brass leather-backed hackney carriage badge, and on Sundays decked themselves with a buttonhole.

In 1892 complaints were made that some of the lads employed as conductors were dirty and ragged "scarcely covering their nakedness", but the company had great difficulty in getting honest and civil conductors. It increased wages and paid 8s. a week to boys of 14 and 15 which was considered high, but the hours were long. The following year a shareholder complained that conductors were still dishonest. On one journey when 5s. was collected, the company only received 2s. 9d. Ticket punches were considered, but the company disliked having to pay the expensive royalty. In 1894 the Directors reported that the conductors were the best since the formation of the company and gave them a day's pay as a Christmas box.

Horses

At first 22 horses were employed. Subsequently 28 horses were shown in the Board of Trade Annual Returns as at 30th June for each year from 1881 to 1884, and 25 at this date from 1885 to 1887, after which the BoT each year from 1888 to 1903 said 'No returns received'. The horses wore a bell on their collar which rang incessantly and drew people's attention to the tram. In summer they wore a 'fan' – wire fixed to the bridle to keep off flies.

Up the gradient of 1 in 16 from the Bell Inn to Walcot Church a trace horse ridden by a man was used; the animal then walked down to Walcot Parade and assisted the inward car up to Walcot Church.

In April 1882, additional tram horses were employed to satisfy the wishes of Bath residents. Horses made two round trips and then as they were passing the stables at the Porter Butt Hotel, they went in for a rest and another pair was put on. The stud consisted of 25 horses when the concern was bought from Dick, Kerr & Co.

In 1892 the horses cost 12s. 9d. each per week to feed, including bedding at 1s. 3d. per head and chaff cutting 4d. A steam engine for cutting chaff cost 1s. 6d. per hour and an economy was made by the company purchasing its own gas engine.

Cars

The six original cars were built by George Starbuck, Birkenhead, seated 18 inside passengers and weighed 33 cwt. The *Bath Chronicle* wrote: 'They are light and airy cars, of attractive appearance, bearing the Bath arms on each side; the furnishing is complete and of the most approved style, providing every comfort for travellers'. They had seven windows, each with curtains and 'Southgate St., Cheap St., High St., Walcot & Grosvenor' painted above them. These six cars were increased to seven before June 1883, but all appear to have been scrapped or sold a year later.

In 1884 the Patent Cable Co. bought seven 1-horse cars seating 12 passengers and weighing only 17½ cwt. They had four windows, coil springs and brake shoes on the leading treads of the wheels. At least on one occasion, a car carried more than 30 passengers to the horse show at Lambridge, people standing on the front and rear platform as well as inside. In Bath the number of passengers was not regulated by the police as in Bristol, where they sometimes turned off passengers to prevent horses being overloaded. On purchase by the Bath Road Car Co. in 1888, the cars were renovated at a cost of £200. They were probably painted blue with a yellow rocker board. A garter with 'Road Car & Tramways Co.' was on the waist panel, together with the number of the car, and 'The Bath Road Car & Tram Co. Limited' on the rocker panel, but later this wording was amended to 'Bath Road Car & Tramway Co. Limited'. The legend above the windows announced 'Southgate St., High St., Walcot & Grosvenor'. The car depot was at the Porter Butt Hotel. One of the cars was kept as a rest room in the Midland coal yard, Bath, for many years.

The conductor was required to light the car lamps when street lights were lit. Bye laws of 1885 required 'The driver of every car shall cause the same to be driven at a speed of not less than four miles an hour on the average, and not exceeding eight miles an hour'. He was not to follow a preceding car at less than 50 yards and need not stop on a gradient of more than 1 in 25. If his line was obstructed, he was to sound his whistle.

Permanent Way

Joseph Kincaid's construction was used and rails laid to a 4 ft gauge. The steel rails were in 24 ft lengths, weighing 32 lb./yd, ⅝ inch in depth to the groove, were set in cast iron chairs at 2 ft 9½ in. centres and tied to gauge every fifth chair. The wrought iron fishplates were 14 in. long. Kincaid used a special type of chair in Cheap Street and other places where cellars under the road did not allow sufficient depth for the ordinary pattern. Before the passing of the 1880 Order and Act the Bath Corporation had laid chairs and the substructure of the tramway in High Street, and a special Schedule attached to this Act said the tramway Promoters must within two months after the passing of the Act repay the £375 costs to the Corporation.

Passing loops, most of which were 3 chains in length, had points of cast steel with a single rocking tongue, and if it was required to take the wrong road, a small lever carried on each car was fitted into a socket on the counterbalance in the switch box.

In streets where stone was allowed, Cornish granite setts were used, 4 in. by 5 in. laid on a bed of gravel on a concrete foundation. Wood blocks were put down elsewhere. The tramway company maintained the road from the GWR station to Grosvenor and saved the city rates at least £240 per annum.

The route length was 1 m. 57 ch.; 41 ch. being double line and 1 m. 16 ch. single with passing places. The Roman Fosse Way was followed fairly closely from Southgate Street to Grosvenor. The terminus at the GWR station had double track, with a 1 chain spur at the Old Bridge for trams terminating there; a loop was opposite St James' Church and another in Stall Street. A further loop was on the corner by the Abbey and a 2 chain section of interlaced track at the bottom of Walcot Street by St Michael's Church. The line continued with a loop at Ladymead, a loop at Cornwell Buildings, an 8 chain loop from Nelson Place to Cleveland Place East, another ordinary short loop at Dover Street; a 2.6 ch. branch to the tram depot by the Porter Butt Hotel, a loop at Kensington Nurseries, another loop at the Balustrade, and the line ended in a single line 1.5 ch. east of the unnamed road between Beaufort Buildings East and West.

Timetable and Fares

In the early days the service had a 10 minute frequency, but by 1900 this had been reduced to one of 15 minutes; the first car from Grosvenor left at 8.30 am (Sundays 2 pm) and the last at 10.30 pm (Sundays 10 pm); while from the GWR station the first car departed at 9.15 am and the last 11.00 pm. On Sundays trams were not allowed along Dorchester Street, and reversed at the bottom of Southgate Street, by the Old Bridge, Sunday departures from here being 2.30–10.30 pm. At a terminus the pin was taken out and the bar, traces and horse were taken round to the other end. This Sunday spur at the Old Bridge was the point where the authorised tramway to Twerton (Nos. 2 & 1 in the 1880 Act) would have started from if built.

The fare was 2d. for the whole distance, and 28 lb. of accompanied luggage was carried free. In 1882 the fare from Walcot Church to the station or Grosvenor was 1d. A waybill was carried inside the tram, and when a passenger boarded the conductor collected the fare and marked an 'X' on the waybill. In later days, tickets were used, as illustrated on *page 3*.

Bath Cable Tramways Car No. 5 at Grosvenor, c.1884. The notice in the left-hand window reads 'Walcot Church to GWR Station One Penny', while that in the right window reads 'Walcot Church to Grosvenor One Penny'. Roof board advertisements are not yet added.   *Author's Collection*

Chapter Two
Electric Cars Begin

Towards the end of 1898 Bath Corporation received letters from the British Electric Traction Co. Ltd and the British Finance & Investment Co. Ltd., who were interested in establishing electric tramways in the City. The BET proposed to apply in May 1899 for a Light Railway Order under the recent 1896 Act, to construct tramways: (1) from Kingsmead Square via Midland Station to Weston with a branch to Newbridge Road, (2) from Old Bridge to Twerton and later through to Newton, and (3) from Old Bridge to Wells Road (St Luke's Church) and later through to Combe Down.

The Corporation was determined that the trams should be under Corporation control, and on 17th December, 1898 formed an Electric Traction Joint Committee to study the subject. In February 1899 it resolved to initiate its own electric tramway system, and to obtain details of costs and operation from other Corporations already owning electric trams. On 23rd March it announced proposals for routes from Old Bridge to Devonshire Buildings, to Upper and Lower Weston, to Twerton, and to Batheaston. Under the 1880 Order the Corporation already had the power to purchase the horse tramways, on 26th August, 1901 (i.e. 21 years after the passing of the 1880 Act) on giving six months notice. In April they resolved to hurry the proceedings, because three companies were now planning rival schemes.

Also in 1899 Drake & Gorham Electric Power & Traction Co. Ltd offered to build a tramway, and the Anderson Electrical Traction Syndicate Ltd wrote on the subject of the closed conduit system of electric traction invented by Christopher Anderson.

In May 1899 the promoters of the Bath & District Light Railways deposited an ambitious plan for 17m. 7f. of lines to Bathford, Combe Down (via Bloomfield Road), Newton (via Lower Bristol Road), Newbridge Hill, Weston (via Julian Road), Lansdown, Camden Road and a loop Claverton Street–Bathwick Street–Henrietta Street, and another loop Bennett Street–the Circus–Upper Church Street. This was modified in November when an extra line to Newton was proposed via Newbridge Road and a branch to Warminster Road. The tram depot was to be on the east side of the destructor works in Upper Bristol Road, and the power station on the west side of the Corporation's power station in Dorchester Street.

Early in 1900, British Electric Traction offered to equip the horse line for electric trams and extend it to Batheaston, Twerton, Devonshire Arms, and Lower Weston, using the Corporation's current; Bath Road Car made application for a similar scheme.

On 8th January, 1900 the Light Railway Commissioners held an Enquiry at Bath into an application by H.T. Ellis, J.W. Davies, and J.F. Hosken for 18 miles of 4 ft gauge tramway extending into the suburbs in six directions, but this was objected to by all the local authorities along the entire route, and hence refused. A rival and very similar scheme was also proposed by Bath Corporation.

On 18th July, 1899 the Corporation had announced it would apply for its own tramway asking for 18 miles of routes to Lansdown, Bathampton, Newbridge, Combe Down via Wells Road, and Newton St Loe via Twerton.

Kingsmead Square at 1.5 pm on 28th February, 1925. Car No. 6 to the Weston Hotel will return from its destination with workers coming back after lunch. The centre car bound for the GWR station, waits in the loop for No. 27 to Weston to clear the single line. The driver of No. 6 assists a passenger across the road. The pole on the right bears three enamel signs: 'Transfer station', 'All cars stop here', and a notice announcing that conductors will accept parcels for delivery.   *Author's Collection*

At a local public enquiry on 9th January, 1900 the Light Railway Commissioners rejected this suggestion as they disapproved of the Corporation spending so much money on seven miles of route outside its own territory. So the Corporation then joined forces with the Promoters of the Bath & District scheme, and in May 1900 application was made jointly by the Mayor, Aldermen, and Citizens of the City and County Borough of Bath, and by Sir James Sivewright and Leopold Hirsch, for a Light Railway Order to incorporate a new company and to sanction the construction of five main routes with several short alternatives in the city centre. These were now to be 4 ft 8½ in. gauge instead of 4 ft, and they totalled 13½ route miles, of which 8¼ miles were inside the City Boundary and 5¼ miles in Bath Rural District, but Lansdown, a very steep hill, was now omitted.

A public enquiry was held by the Light Railway Commissioners at Bath on 30th July, 1900, and almost everything that had been asked for was granted, except that the Corporations's two requests for the new company to be allowed to run motor buses on certain roads, and for it to have to pay an annual rental for the use of city streets, were both refused. On 5th December, 1900 supplementary plans were deposited asking for an 18-chain extension to the Lower Bristol Road route at Twerton. The amended Order was approved and submitted to the Board of Trade on 9th May, 1901, and confirmed by the Board on 2nd November, 1901, as their Order No. 132. The only serious objectors had been the governors of King Edward's School, who disliked the site of the proposed power station in Walcot Street so near their premises.

The Bath and District Light Railways Order of 1901 thus incorporated a new Bath and District Light Railway Company, as a body corporate with perpetual succession, with five Directors, who were specified as 'Sir James Sivewright and Leopold Hirsch and three other persons to be nominated by them', and they each had to possess at least £250 of the share capital. The capital of the company was to be £225,000 in £1 shares, with borrowing powers of £75,000, and the Order authorised it to construct all the following light railways, with all proper rails, plates, works, and conveniences connected therewith:

> No. 1 (1 mile 52 chains), from the terminus of the existing horse tramway opposite the main entrance to Bath GWR station, along Dorchester Street, Southgate Street, Stall Street, Cheap Street, High Street, Northgate Street, Walcot Street, Ladymead, Cornwell Buildings, London Street, Fosse Way, and London Road, to end near the terminus of the existing tramway opposite Grosvenor Place at Lambridge, 'provided that the said railway shall not be constructed until the existing tramway has been removed'.
>
> No. 1A (2 miles 2 chains), continuing onwards further along London Road and High Street Batheaston north-eastwards, then south-eastwards along Stambridge Place, and under the bridge carrying the GWR main line, to end in the main road to Melksham near the Crown Inn at Bathford.
>
> No. 1B (19 chains), continuing further along the Melksham Road to end near the New Inn at Bathford, provided that 1B must not be constructed except in connection with a further extension which would allow the line to terminate on a suitable gradient, and also only if Bath Rural District Council ask the Company to

use their best endeavours to obtain the necessary powers to make such extension. [This was because the road through Bathford was up a very steep hill, as well as being narrow and twisty. Many years later, in 1956, a motor bus did lose control here, and crashed through a wall and overturned.]

No. 1C (35 chains), from a junction with No. 1 in Northgate Street, to run via Broad Street, Bladud Buildings, The Paragon, and Somerset Buildings, to rejoin No. 1 in London Street.

No. 2 (50 chains), starting in Weston Lane near its junction with High Street Weston then passing southwards along Weston Lane and Combe Park to end in Newbridge Hill at its junction with Kelston Road.

No. 2A (28 chains), starting in Newbridge Road (Lower Weston) close to east end of Quarry (i.e. at Newbridge Park), passing eastwards along Newbridge Road to end in Upper Bristol Road by a junction with No. 2B near the Weston Hotel.

No. 2B (1 mile 41 chains), from a junction with No. 2 in Newbridge Hill, then along Upper Bristol Road, Monmouth Place, Monmouth Street, Westgate Buildings, St James's Parade, and Corn Street, to join No. 1 in Southgate Street.

No. 2C (49 chains), alternative route into the city centre from Upper Bristol Road, via Nile Street, Great Stanhope Street, New King Street, Kingsmead Street, Kingsmead Square, Avon Street, and Corn Street, to rejoin No. 2B opposite St James's Parade.

No. 3 (1 mile 58 chains) (the original application plus the extension at Twerton), starting in Lower Bristol Road at Twerton one chain east of a connecting road leading to Twerton High Street, then along Lower Bristol Road to end at the southern end of Old Bridge.

No. 3A (3.5 chains), across Old Bridge from No. 3 to join No. 1 in Southgate Street.

No. 3B (0.5 chains), a curve from 3A to join No. 1 in Dorchester Street.

No. 4 (18 chains), starting at Oldfield Park in Cynthia Road opposite Bridge Road, then along Cynthia Road and Herbert Road to end near the Livingstone Hotel.

No. 4A (47 chains), continuing from the end of No. 4 along Livingstone Road, Lower Oldfield Park, and Westmoreland Road, to join No. 3 in Lower Bristol Road.

No. 5 (52.25 chains), starting in the main road at Combe Down opposite the Convalescent Home on the corner of Shaft Road, then westwards along the main road (Bradford Road) to end 26 chains west from the Hadley Arms public house.

No. 5A (59.60 chains), continuing further west along Bradford Road to end near Glasshouse Farm.

No. 5B (1 mile 78 chains), continuing northwards from here along the road in front of the Bath Union Workhouse (Midford Road), then along the main Wells Road to join No. 3 at the approach to Old Bridge.

No. 6 (28.5 chains), starting in Dorchester Street by a junction with No. 1 outside Bath Railway Station, then via Manvers Street, Pierrepont Street, North Parade, Terrace Walk, and the north side of Orange Grove, to rejoin No. 1 in High Street near the Guildhall, i.e. the route that had been rejected in 1880.

This gave a total of 13 miles 61.35 chains (including the 18-chain afterthought) but no mention was made as to which should be single track and which double. The gauge was to be 4 ft 8½ in. If the Company could acquire at reasonable cost the necessary land, they were, at their own expense, to widen certain specified parts of Nos. 5 and 5A to not less than 23 feet and then dedicate it to the public as a highway. The company was given power to acquire and remove the existing horse tramway, but only by agreement, and so as not to prejudice the existing rights of the Bath Road Car & Tramways Co. Ltd.

The Order gave the company power to build a power station and generate electricity, on a plot of ground in the parish of Walcot located between Walcot Street and the River Avon in the Beehive Yard just north of the corn market and cattle market. This power station was built on a site previously occupied by part of the Walcot iron and brass foundry, and an eight-road car shed was built between the power station and the corn market on a site previously occupied by a malthouse and its outhouses. For this and similar purposes the company was authorised to purchase by agreement, or to sell, up to not more than 10 acres of land. The powers for compulsory purchase of land needed for the tramways were to cease after three years from the date of the Order, but another Clause tells us that if the whole of the railway is not completed within three years from the date of the Order the powers shall cease, though the Board of Trade could allow an extension of time if it thought fit.

'When constructing or maintaining the tramway the company must not open or break up at any one time a greater length than 100 yards of any road which does not exceed a quarter mile in length, nor on longer roads leave a less interval than a quarter mile between any two such places, and all such works must be completed within four weeks and the surface made good.' Subsequently the Company was required at its own expense to keep in good repair the road surface between the rails and for 18 inches either side. Power was given to alter single track to double or vice versa, subject to the approval of the road authority, or to fix overhead wires to buildings instead of erecting posts or standards, or for the local authority to fix its street lighting lamps to the tramway poles without payment. No siding or passing place was to be built within 10 yards either side of the entrance to the GWR goods station in Lower Bristol Road, and no tramway carriage was to stop in this section for longer than absolutely necessary for taking up and setting down traffic.

Powers for compulsory purchase of the tramways, by Bath Corporation for the portion inside the City, and by Somerset County Council for the portion inside Bath Rural District, were fixed as being within six months after 32 years from the date when the Board of Trade certified the railway or any part of it to be fit for traffic, or within six months after every subsequent 10 years. This date was later fixed as being 13th January, 1936, and was instead of the more usual 21 years and then every seven years of most other tramways elsewhere. If the County Council did not want to purchase its portion this too could then be purchased by Bath Corporation. The company could also sell the undertaking voluntarily to the City Corporation and the County Council at any earlier date. Also, having started to construct the routes, if the company failed to complete them before a date to be fixed by the Board of Trade, they could be purchased and completed by the Corporation of the County Council. After any of these purchasing methods the buyer was then empowered to lease the tramways to anybody else. If a route was not used for three months its powers would then expire, and the Local Authority could remove it, although in practice running just one car in three months was enough to maintain the rights.

Passenger fares from the Guildhall were not to exceed 1d. to the Railway Tavern at Twerton, to Newbridge Park at Lower Weston, to the corner of Gloucester Road at Larkhall, to the Oldfield Park terminus, or to Portway

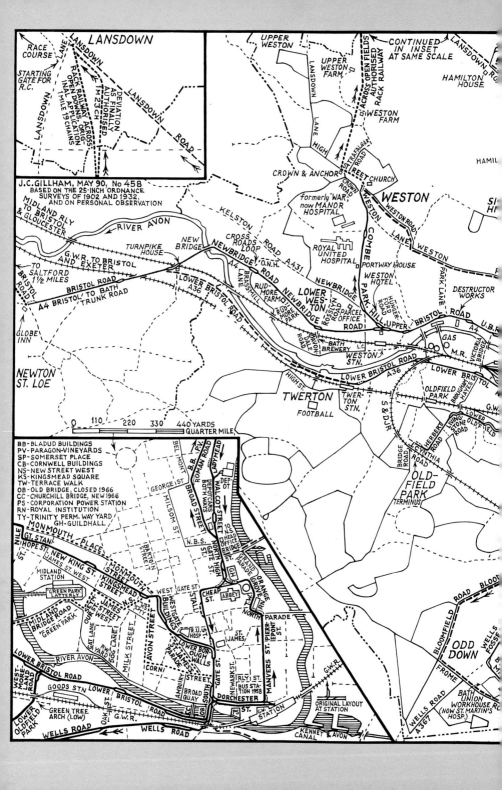

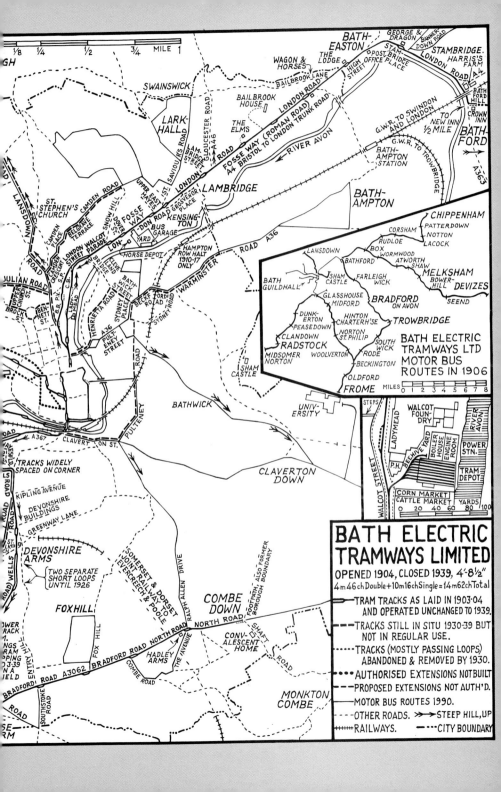

House at Combe Park, and not to exceed 2d. to Batheaston Post Office, and not to exceed 3d. to the Convalescent Home at Combe Down or to the Crown Inn at Bathford, and not to exceed 4d. to the New Inn at Bathford. Fares were not to be higher on Sundays, and Workmen's fares were to be available on weekdays before 8 am and after 5 pm.

A new company, called Bath Electric Tramways Limited, was formed on 9th July, 1902, with registered offices at 18 St Helen's Place, London, EC, and quotations on the London stock exchange. There were five Directors, who, after a few early changes, were (1) Sir Vincent Caillard (Chairman), of Piccadilly, London, who was also Chairman of Beyer Peacock & Co. Ltd, the Manchester locomotive builders; (2) Evelyn Henry Raynward Trenow (Managing), of London; (3) the Hon. Sir James Sivewright, KCMG, LLD, MIEE, of Cape Town, South Africa; (4) A.A. Campbell Swinton, MICE, MIEE, of Victoria, London, who was also the managing director of the electricity supply companies at Cambridge and Scarborough; and (5) Hugh Frank Clutterbuck, a local man living at Bath. The Secretary was Harry James Almond, also Secretary of the Sunderland District Electric Tramways Limited (SDET). The SDET also shared the same offices at 18 St Helen's Place, and one of the SDET directors was E. (not V.) Caillard, such an unusual name indicating there must have been some connection between the Bath and Sunderland tramways. The general manager and Engineer at Walcot Street, Bath, was R.D. McCarter. The authorised capital of the new Bath company was 75,000 5 per cent preference shares of £1 each, plus 155,000 ordinary shares of £1 each, total £230,000, of which £180,606 was issued.

By an Indenture dated 3rd April, 1903 the undertaking of the Bath & District Light Railway Company was transferred to the Bath Electric Tramways Ltd, which one month later applied for another Light Railway Order. This was duly approved, and confirmed by the Board of Trade on 18th September, 1903 as the Bath Electric Tramways (Light Railway Extensions) Order of 1903, Order No. 197. This authorised the abandonment of the construction of the portions of railway No. 2B in the 1901 Order located in Monmouth Place, Monmouth Street, St James's Parade, and Corn Street (but not Westgate Buildings), and also of the portion of 2C of 1901 located in Avon Street and Corn Street. Nos. 2B and 2C had in any case always been intended as alternatives, and the effect now was that a part of each was scrapped and a part of each survived. Compensation was now to be paid to the owner or occupier of lands on the abandoned sections for damage that had been caused in surveying, taking levels, probing, boring to find the nature of the soil, or setting out the lines of route, but the new tramway company was released from the Contracts which the old company had entered into for the purchase of these lands.

The 1903 Order also authorised construction of three short new sections:

> No. 3 (32.5 chains), starting in Lower Bristol Road by a junction with No. 3 of 1901, then into and along the road leading to the Midland railway station, across Midland Bridge over the River Avon, along Seymour Street, past the front of the Midland (Green Park) station, and along James Street and New Street to join No. 2C of 1901 in Kingsmead Square.

Certificate for five Preferred Ordinary Shares in Bath Electric Tramways Limited issued to Henry Hinton, 34, The Triangle, Oldfield Park, Bath on 28th October, 1902. Henry Hinton was a carpenter and builder.

Author's Collection

Nº 045

PREFERENCE TO THE DEFERRED ORDINARY SHARES, AND AFTER PAYMENT THEREOF, SUBJECT TO DIRECTORS
REMUNERATION, TO ONE-HALF OF THE PROFITS REMAINING IN EACH YEAR.

THE BATH ELECTRIC TRAMWAYS LIMITED

CAPITAL £230,000

Incorporated under the
Companies Acts 1862 to 1900

DIVIDED INTO

75,000 5% Cumulative Preference Shares of £1 each   Nos 1 to 75,000
125,000 Preferred Ordinary Shares of £1 each   Nos 75001 to 200,000
and 30,000 Deferred Ordinary Shares of £1 each   Nos 200001 to 230,000

PREFERRED ORDINARY SHARES.

THESE PREFERRED ORDINARY SHARES ARE PREFERRED AS TO CAPITAL OVER THE DEFERRED ORDINARY SHARES.

This is to Certify that Henry Hinton Esq., Builder
of The Triangle, Oldfield Park, Bath
is the registered holder of Five   Preferred Ordinary Shares
numbered   86657 — to 86661 —   inclusive in the above named Company
subject to the Memorandum and Articles of Association thereof and that the
sum of seven shillings sixpence   has been paid up upon each of the said Shares

Given under the Common Seal of the said Company
this   28th   day of October   1902.

The Common Seal of the said Company
was hereunto affixed in the presence of

                                        DIRECTOR.

                                        SECRETARY.

NOTE.—NO TRANSFER OF ANY PORTION OF THE SHARES COMPRISED IN THIS CERTIFICATE WILL BE
REGISTERED UNTIL THE CERTIFICATE HAS BEEN DELIVERED AT THE OFFICES OF THE COMPANY.

N.B. THIS RECEIPT IS TO BE DETACHED AND FORWARDED TO THE SECRETARY AT THE OFFICES OF THE COMPANY.

BATH ELECTRIC TRAMWAYS LIMITED.

Nº 045

Received the certificate bearing this number for Five
Preferred Ordinary Shares in the above company.

Signature
Address at Triangle, Oldfield Park, Bath

Date   19

No. 3A (1.10 chains), a short junction line in Kingsmead Square from 2C of 1901 to join 2B of 1901 in Westgate Buildings.

No. 4 (8.8 chains), from 2B of 1901 in Westgate Buildings, along Lower Borough Walls, to join No. 1 of 1901 in Southgate Street.

This Lower Borough Walls link was an alternative to St James's Parade of 1901, now abandoned. No. 3 was not to be built unless the Corporation gave its consent within six months of the Order, and also not until Midland Bridge had been widened or rebuilt. The powers for 3A and 4 were to expire in two years. In fact No. 3 never was built, although 3A & 4 were. Nos. 1 and 2 were deleted from the May 1903 application, but they had been for a line from the top of Broad Street to the Hare & Hounds at Lansdown: 1 m 25 ch of gradients 1 in 7–18, and a line along Julian Road to Weston to connect at Weston with a proposed Bath & Lansdown Light Railway. Extremely detailed and restrictive conditions were laid down in the 1903 Order, also applying to all the tramways of 1901, for the protection of the Postmaster-General and his telegraphic lines from the injurious effects of stray currents from the electrical circuits of the tramways and overhead wires. The rails in Lower Borough Walls opposite the Royal United Hospital were to be laid on longitudinal sleepers of wood, and cars were not to be allowed to stop there, nor to pass one another, nor sound any bells or gongs unless absolutely necessary for safety.

The Bath Tramways Company agreed to pay two-thirds (£8,400) of the cost of the new Midland Bridge required over the river, and though this money was paid, cars never used this bridge, as the company was not allowed to run trams in Westgate Street. Rails were laid on the bridge itself to avoid disturbing the new road surface if the line was required. Westgate Street if sanctioned would have provided a valuable link from Midland Bridge direct to Cheap Street and High Street.

George Hopkins & Son and Harper Bros. & Co. were Engineers to the Bath Electric Tramways. The contract for the permanent way and overhead was let to Charles Chadwell, Victoria Street, London, while British Westinghouse Electric & Manufacturing Co. Ltd won the contract for the generating station, car shed, and fitting out the cars, and this latter company carried out its contract in the record time of less than 7½ months.

Work on the permanent way began at Cornwell Buildings, Walcot Street, in November 1902 and gave employment to idle men in the City, who were paid 4½d. an hour and worked 12 hours a day wielding a 14 lb. sledgehammer. In March 1903 the rails in London Street were found to be at the wrong level and had to be lowered. As London Street was blocked, the Cleveland Bridge was thrown open free of toll, and the proprietors were paid £35 for the first week and £30 for subsequent weeks. Half the cost of this was paid by the contractors and half by the city. This mistake in levels gave the city extra expense as the bridge had to be toll-free for longer than intended.

As was usually the case with laying tramways, BET (Bath Electric Tramways) were not allowed to break up more than 100 yards in each quarter of a mile of road and had to restore it within four weeks; but the city surveyor allowed the company to open a greater length than this, as he thought it better that work progressed quickly in the summer when Bath had fewer visitors, than to have the work still going on in autumn, winter and spring when the Season was in progress.

In August 1903 it was pointed out that rails were too near the Guildhall entrance and there was no room for carriages to stand. The same criticism applied in Stall Street outside the principal entrance to the Baths. These alterations involved the BET in several hundreds of pounds of additional expense. Most of the frontage owners in narrow streets agreed to rosettes being fixed to their premises, avoiding cumbersome standards.

For such apparently simple matters such as fixing a rosette to the wall of Bath railway station, erecting four trolley poles to carry the wires under the railway bridge at Batheaston, installing wooden troughing underneath Old-field Park railway bridge, and placing just one pole on railway land at the Broad Quay, Bath station, and Twerton station, the Tramway company had to enter into four separate Agreements, each of several pages, with the Great Western Railway, and pay Government Stamp Duty on each.

By early September only 1¼ miles of track remained unlaid, and it was expected that trams would start in November. Hopes were dashed as the power station was not quite ready, though in mid-November the tall steel chimney was finished and its completion marked by American and British flags being flown from the top. Power station plant arrived at the Midland Railway station and was taken to the site on low-loaders drawn by traction engines. The cars arrived in early December, and were electrically equipped at the depot, while the work of connecting it to Walcot Street was in progress.

Col Von Donop, himself a Bathonian, made the Board of Trade inspection on 12th December, 1903. Six cars were expected to arrive at the Guildhall at 9.45 am, and convey the officers over the system, but they did not materialise as a pump at the power station had failed. At 10.30 carriages and pairs were drawn up outside the Guildhall, and part of the system was inspected using this method of transport. Later in the day, the fault corrected, they ran over the whole system by tram. Initially the BET advertised for motormen from other tramway concerns, and when the system was working, trained its own conductors to become motormen.

The regular service began on 2nd January, 1904 when at 11 am the first of the double-deckers left for Bathford. There was a rush for seats, but plenty of police were on duty. The next car ran to Twerton, the following one to Devonshire Arms and then one to Weston. On the first day an average of 17 out of the 20 available cars carried 22,800 passengers. The following day only 15 cars were running due to slight breakdown. There had thus been an interval of 18 months between the last horse tram and the first electric tram.

A low bridge in Westmoreland Road on the Oldfield Park route necessi-tated single-deck cars, and this was not opened at first as the company had only received two of the four cars ordered. The service was eventually started on Saturday afternoon 23rd January, still with only two cars, and these ran from the GWR station; the Guildhall could not be used as a terminus as the line up through the town was too heavily used by the two-way existing tram traffic. It was obvious that the situation would have to be eased by building a Manvers Street/Pierrepoint Street line to the Guildhall.

This idea was strengthened when in February, 1,087 Oldfield Park residents sent a deputation to the City Council, which had stipulated that the BET should convey passengers from Oldfield Park to the Guildhall for 1d., yet passengers were being 'dumped down at the GWR station'. R.D. McCarter, the manager, said that if the Council sanctioned the Pierrepont Street route, Oldfield Park cars would go to the Guildhall. By the end of April, standards and rails were being put in and notices posted notifying the closure of Manvers and Pierrepont Streets to vehicles for about three weeks.

This tramway as built had to make a detour via North Parade and Terrace Walk, with three sharp corners, because the Royal Literary and Scientific Institution (built 1824) blocked the direct route. Although this building was demolished in 1936, and the present-day straight road (Parade Gardens) constructed, the tramway was never diverted.

The line opened on 14th July, 1904, formed a terminal loop for Twerton and Oldfield Park cars and a one way system for those on the Combe Down–Bathford service. All cars thus now normally worked northbound via Manvers Street and southbound via Southgate Street, although in fact there were passing loops on both routes and they could both be used either way. Similarly Broad Street was normally used northbound only and Walcot Street southbound only, though either could be used either way in an emergency, and empty trams returning to the depot each night always used Walcot Street northbound.

The terminus for Combe Down trams was temporarily Devonshire Arms, but at a very early date it was extended to the Workhouse, 530 ft above sea level; but completion to Combe Down was delayed because of a dispute with the local authority over road widening. The BET had offered £16,400 for the Corporation to build the new Midland Bridge and widen all necessary roads in the city and district, but a quibble occurred. The line was eventually opened on 31st July, 1904 when the temporary BET horse bus service Workhouse–Convalescent Home ceased operation. Everything sanctioned in the 1901 Order, as modified by the 1903 Order, was now complete, except that the outer end of the Bathford route from the Crown Inn to the New Inn never was built. Meanwhile the official opening ceremony of the tramways took place on 13th February, having been postponed until work on the power station had been completed. Visitors looked at the power station; then Lady Caillard, wife of Sir Vincent Caillard, Chairman of the BET (and four months later appointed Director of the London, Chatham & Dover Railway), took the motorman's place at the front of a car in the depot, and declared the tramways open. A luncheon followed in the Banqueting Room of the Guildhall, attended by the Directors, Engineers, Mayor and Corporation, together with representatives of numerous electrical and tramway journals.

Another Light Railway Order was applied for in November 1904 by the company, and so the Bath Electric Tramways (Light Railway Extensions) Order of 1905 was duly sanctioned by the Board of Trade on 18th July, 1905, as BoT Order No. 246. It authorised, as No. 1, an extension of 1 mile 59 chains in Bath Rural District, from the terminus of the existing line at Avondale Road in Newbridge Road, Lower Weston, further along Newbridge

Road, over the New Bridge itself into the Keynsham Rural District, crossing the Midland Railway's Mangotsfield to Bath branch and the GWR's Bristol to London main line. It continued along the Bristol Road to terminate at the Globe Inn at the crossroads a little to the north of the village of Newton St Loe. Three years were given for completion, before the powers expired, with a fine of £20 per day for every day after 18th July, 1908 that the line was not open. This 1905 Order brought the total so far authorised to 16 miles 2.75 chains, but meanwhile 32.5 chains of the 1901 powers had lapsed through non-construction, and 51 chains through authorised abandonment, also 19 chains No. 1B (see page 19).

The opening of the extension from Newbridge Park to Newton on 5th August, 1905 at a cost of £11,300, completed the system totalling 14.78 miles. Nine thousand passengers travelled to Newton in the first week, this figure gradually declining to give an average of 2,860. In the first 21 weeks the extension carried 60,000 passengers, weekly receipts averaging £32 10s. To a stranger, the line seemed to end in the country miles from anywhere, but actually it was only a quarter of a mile from the villages of Newton St Loe and Corston. The Newton route proved that a good income was to be had from people wanting a trip to get country air so a further extension to Saltford was proposed, probably with the eventual link-up with Bristol Tramways also in mind, for that company was intending to extend to Keynsham, and this would have left only a gap of two miles between the systems. Saltford was a popular boating centre, and McCarter expected the journey would take 35 minutes from Bath by tram. The cost of construction would have been low — only £17,000 including electrical equipment. The population of Saltford was 547, and the BET expected to carry 200–400 passengers a day; many would have been joy-riders only going to the terminus and not getting off the car.

A Light Railway inquiry was held at the Guildhall on 27th January, 1906 when Newton and Saltford were for the application, which was only opposed by the Somerset County Council and the Keynsham Rural District Council. The Order was granted on 18th August, 1906, as the Bath Electric Tramways (Light Railway Extensions) Order of 1906, BoT No. 276, and it authorised the construction of:

> No. 1 (1 mile 23½ chains), continuing from the Globe Inn north-westwards along the main Bristol Road as far as a point half a chain south of the approach entrance to Saltford GWR station in the parish of Saltford and the Rural District of Keynsham.
> No. 2 (23½ chains), continuing still further along the Bristol Road as far as the Crown Inn at Saltford.

Three years from the date of the Order were again set for expiry of the power if not yet started, or the £20 per day fine if nearly finished. The Order was signed by David Lloyd George, President of the Board of Trade.

Preparations were made to start the Saltford extension as soon as a favourable opportunity arose, but unfortunately the weather in 1907 was poor and receipts fell, and owing to the poor state of the money market, the extension was never built. In February 1907 the Bristol Tramways & Carriage Co. Ltd inaugurated a motor bus service eleven times daily from its Brislington tram terminus via Keynsham and Saltford to the Globe Inn at Newton, with through tickets from Bristol to Bath via Bristol trams, Bristol buses, and Bath tramcars.

Meanwhile on 28th April, 1905 a company called Projects Limited had been registered, with offices at Parliament Mansions, Great Smith Street, London, SW, and an authorised capital of £2,000, of which only £544 was issued by 1906. There were three Directors, H.L. Godden, R.H. Pearson, and Major R.W. McKay by 1906, all of whom lived in London. Neither these three, nor the company itself, had any other connections with tramways or anything similar elsewhere in Britain apart from Bath, so far as is known, though they did have ambitious hopes of applying for Bills or Orders for railways or tramways or electric power stations in various locations.

In Bath they proposed a double-centre rack railway with a maximum gradient of 1-in-4 from Weston tram terminus to Lansdown, which would have been useful for racegoers and other pleasure traffic. Lansdown is 740 feet above sea level and there had been several previous tramway proposals to reach it by other routes. Project deposited plans in May 1905 for 1 mile 19 chains of double line on an independent right of way from the Crown & Anchor Inn, Weston, to the top of Lansdown Lane, and also 13.75 chains of street tramway to link with the existing Bath Tramways terminus at Manor Road. Running powers over the street section were to be given to Bath Tramways, with powers to purchase after five years. The Engineers were to be Godden & Co., and the estimated cost of construction for the entire scheme, including an independent power station, was £14,500. The intention was to have separate rack locomotives to push tramcars up the hill.

The Light Railway Commissioners held an enquiry at the Bath Guildhall in June 1905. The Commissioners present at the opening of the enquiry were the Hon A.E. Gathorne-Hardy and Colonel G.F.O. Boughey, RE, CSI, with Mr Alan D. Erskine as Secretary, later they were joined by Mr H.A. Steward. For the promoters Mr Mitchell-Innes said the total length of the proposed railway was 1 m., 33.75 chains. Motive power would be electricity, on the overhead trolley system, which at first would be taken from the Bath Electric Tramways Co. Ltd, under arrangement. The gauge would be 4 ft 8½ in., and the proposed capital was £15,000. Mr Harry Luttrell Godden, Engineer to the promoters, considered the rack railway quite practicable. He proposed fitting the electric motor in a bogie so that any rolling and pitching of the car body would not disconnect the pinion from the rack.

He thought the speed should be limited to about 6¾ mph for safety. He calculated that an average of 400 passengers would be carried daily and a return fare of 4d. would allow a dividend of 7½ per cent to be declared. People from the city would be able to go to Lansdown and back for about 6d., which was different from paying 6s. for a slow cab journey.

The Chairman said the Commissioners were prepared to sanction this line if they could be satisfied that the promoters were able to widen one narrow point. If that could be cleared up to their satisfaction they were prepared to grant the Order. The application for a Light Railway Order was therefore slightly amended in November 1905 to give a straighter line, and the estimated cost was raised to £17,573.

The revised application was approved, and confirmed by the Board of Trade on 9th August, 1906, as the Bath & Lansdown Light Railways Order of 1906, the BoT No. 274. It incorporated the Bath and Lansdown Light Railway Company, as a body corporate with perpetual succession, an authorised capital of £18,000 in 18,000 shares of £1 each, also powers to borrow up to £6,000 on mortgage. Its offices were at 23 New Bond Street, Bath. There were to be five Directors, namely the three Directors of Projects Limited and two other persons to be nominated by them. The Order authorised:

No. 1 (1 mile 23 chains), wholly in the Rural District of Bath, starting in the parish and village of Weston 3.75 chains west of Trafalgar Road thence in a northerly direction through open lands and fields and between Weston Farm and Upper Weston Farm, thence in a north-westerly direction to end near the intersection of Lansdown Hill with Lansdown Road just a little short of Lansdown itself. This line was to be constructed and maintained with a rack rail, subject to the approval of the Board of Trade. The Order said 'The Company may . . . carry the same with a single line only whilst it shall consist of a single line and afterwards with a double line only across and on the level of any private road . . . except where a station or stopping place adjoins such private road . . . and there the Company may also lay down such additional lines as may be necessary to provide for trains passing each other at the station or stopping place.' [This implies single track with passing loops, but the Board of Trade Annual Returns for the next five years afterwards, under the heading of Authorised but not built, all say double line 1 m. 37 ch., single line nil.]

No. 2 (13.75 chains), a conventional street tramway, starting by a junction with the bottom of No. 1, then passing eastwards along High Street Weston to end in Weston Lane by a junction with the existing tramway of Bath Electric Tramways. Before building this tramway the company was required to widen the High Street at its own expense and to acquire the land necessary for this.

The company was authorised to erect a generating station and to supply energy, or to purchase power from any other source and the gauge was to be 4 ft 8½ in. The powers for the compulsory purchase of land were to expire three years after the date of the Order, and for completion of all the works five years after the date of the Order. As to rates and tolls, the company could charge as for three miles the 1¼ miles up the hill on Railway No. 1, but on No. 2 the fares, etc., would be the same as on Bath Tramways. Bath Electric Tramways Limited was given power to operate Railway No. 2, along Weston High Street, on payment of tolls.

It could also require the Lansdown company to sell them this portion, in which case the Lansdown company would not be allowed to apply for any Act or Order for any further extension of its line except for not more than half a mile on the top of Lansdown Hill.

Somerset County Council was given power to purchase Railway No. 2, but if Bath Corporation should have purchased, or given notice to purchase, the

Weston tramway in the 1901 Order then the Corporation and not the County could instead purchase the Railway No. 2. Any time after five years from the date when No. 2 was to be certified by the Board of Trade to be fit for traffic Bath Tramways could, if it still owned the Weston route, now also purchase Railway No. 2. Any time after 20 years (not 21) from the date when No. 1 was to be certified by the BoT as fit for traffic Bath Tramways could, if still the owner of the Weston line and also now the owner of No. 2, or having served notice to purchase No. 2, then it could also purchase Railway No. 1.

For any sale before 14th January, 1933 the purchase price was to be the fair market value as a going concern, but for any sale after 13th January the price was to be as per Section 43 of the Tramways Act of 1870. Neither Bath Corporation nor Somerset County Council would be allowed to purchase Railway No. 2 unless it had already purchased the 1901 Weston line. Additionally the Lansdown company was not allowed to sell its undertaking without previously offering it to Bath Corporation at the same price. If and when the whole undertaking was sold the Company could then be wound up, and if the Corporation or the County Council acquired the undertaking they could lease it to anybody else.

However, the scheme proved abortive, and construction was never started and the powers expired in August 1911. What might have been the only rack railway in Britain apart from Snowdon never came to pass, and the Promoters lost a considerable sum in surveying the land and obtaining the Light Railway Order. Both the Lansdown company and Projects Limited then vanished without trace, and already by 1908 the trade directories say for both companies: 'letters returned marked gone away'.

Returning to Bath Electric Tramways, it applied in May 1908 for another Light Railway Order, but no route extensions were involved. This was approved, after a local Public Enquiry at Bath on 18th July, 1908, submitted to the Board of Trade on 28th October, 1908, and confirmed by them on 12th January, 1909, as the Bath Electric Tramways (Light Railway Amendment) Order of 1909, BoT Order No. 327. This one was signed by Winston S. Churchill, President of the Board of Trade, and dealt with two subjects only.

One was fare stages on the Upper Bristol Road route. The 1901 Order had fixed the fares (amongst others) from Guildhall to Avondale Road (Lower Weston terminus), and to Portway House (Combe Park) at 1d. each. The 1909 Order cancelled this, and instead fixed at 1d. each: GWR station to Park Lane, Park Lane to Cross Roads loop (Newbridge Road), Park Lane to Upper Weston terminus and Kingsmead Square to Weston Hotel; at 1½d. each, GWR station to Rudmore Farm (Newbridge Road), and GWR station to Upper Weston terminus. On Bank Holidays and days on which Bath race meetings were held these two 1½d. fares could be increased to 2d. The 1909 Order also granted powers to fix fare stages on any route so that each two consecutive stages should be not less than a mile long, and no stage should be less than one-third of a mile long.

The other subject was to give the Postmaster-General powers to fix telegraph or telephone wires on the tramway posts, standards and brackets, with protective Clauses and details of how to pay for them. All such wires were to be fixed to the posts or brackets below the level of the trolley wires and on the side of the posts farthest from the trolley wires, but no such wires were to be fixed to any centre poles, and nothing in this new telegraph permission removed the existing right of the local authority of using the tramway poles or brackets for street lighting.

Motor Bus Feeder Service

As early as 1900 when the electric trams were mooted, motor buses were proposed for the hilly districts. Late in 1904, McCarter decided to adopt motor buses to feed the tramways and the first Milnes-Daimler was delivered in August 1905. Six Milnes-Daimler FB 02–07 and six Straker-Squires FB 08–13 were delivered. The former seated 32 and the latter 35, roller doors were fitted to both types. The six Milnes-Daimlers cost a total of £7,300 and the Straker-Squires £8,000. York Villa was bought for £2,200 and the grounds used as the site of the bus garage. In 1906 the bus mileage was 163,139 with a route mileage of 76¼; they 'rather more than paid their own way and acted as very valuable feeders to the tramway system'. The Milnes-Daimlers had double-deck bodywork by Christopher Dodson of Willesden, and the Straker-Squires bodies of the same unusual design, but built by the Bristol Wagon & Carriage Works Co. Ltd.

By 1908 buses were working ten times a day from the Guildhall to Lansdown Road, of which three per day continued up the hill to Lansdown Golf Club, 3 miles distant. Fares were 1d. to Julian Road, 2d. to St Stephen's Church, 3d. to Hamilton Road, 4d. to Hamilton House, and 6d. to the Golf Club. Six buses ran daily from the Guildhall to Sham Castle Golf Club in the south-eastern suburbs, 2 miles away. Most of the Bath Tramways buses, however, worked country routes, not from the city centre, but from points near the outer ends of two of the tram routes.

The Straker-Squires ran mainly from Bathford, and the Milnes-Daimlers from Glasshouse, as the latter were better at climbing gradients. The transfer point at Bathford was in the middle of the main road junction (A4 and A363 today) just before the railway bridge, and a large notice fixed to the tramway pole alongside the signpost read 'Alight Here for Motor Omnibuses'. At Glasshouse Farm adjacent to the cross-roads of Bradford Road and Midford Road, the Tramways Company owned a Cafe and Tea Gardens for use by passengers transferring from tram to bus or vice versa.

Three bus routes were worked from Bathford, but only from May to October. These were Bathford–Box–Corsham–Lacock–Chippenham, 13 miles, Wed./Sat./Sun. only, three or four journeys; Bathford–Box–Atworth–Melksham–Seend–Devizes, 17 miles, Tue./Thur./Sat./Sun. only, three or four journeys; Bathford–Bradford–Trowbridge–Beckington–Frome, 16 miles, Mon./Wed./Sat. only, two or three journeys. The two routes from Glasshouse worked all the year round, and were Glasshouse–Midford–Norton St Philip–Beckington–Frome, 11 miles, daily, three to five journeys, also Glasshouse–Dunkerton–Radstock–Midsomer Norton, 10 miles, Mon./Tue./Wed./Sat./Sun., three to five journeys.

With a fleet of 12 buses spare vehicles were available for working private-hire trips, which often went further afield. Every Monday a horse-brake left Frome at 12.30 soon after arrival of the bus from Bath via Trowbridge, for a four-hour drive around Longleat and Shearwater at an inclusive tram–bus–brake return fare of 4s. 6d. Circular trips were also run during the summer to Stonehenge, Cheddar, Portishead, and Clevedon. Motor coach excursions with Commer Car and Dennis charabancs were inaugurated in 1912, and developed extensively in the 1920s. In November 1929 the bus services formerly starting from the Glasshouse were extended into the city to start from the Old Bridge, and similarly those formerly starting at Bathford were extended to the Grand Parade. All the new routes inaugurated subsequently also terminated at the Grand Parade, except for those to the south and south-west, which still used the Old Bridge.

Personalities

An American, R.D. McCarter, was the first General Manager, and stayed until 30th June, 1908 to get the tramway working. He was then retained as consulting engineer, and his deputy, William Eversley Hardy, took over. S.L. de Ferranti wrote the letter of recommendation by which he got the job at Bath in 1903. Hardy was well-liked by his men and all said 'He was a gentleman'. He would work with them getting snow off the track and went to the station and welcomed them home after demobilisation. On the death of J.B. Hamilton in 1925, he was appointed Managing Director. Hardy was a prominent member of the Tramways & Light Railways Association.

Edward Seckington was the traffic (commercial) superintendent and Rowley the first chief inspector, who was succeeded by Daniel Evry in 1910 and Albert Hale in 1933. William Gilbert Cresham Adams was the chief clerk and cashier in 1913, accountant and commercial superintendent in 1919 and Assistant Manager in 1928. William John Targett was appointed engine driver in 1903 and promoted engineer in charge of the power station in 1909. Radcliffe Dodd came to the company as fitter and was made general superintendent in 1928.

Chapter Three
From 1910 Onwards

In 1911 the Directors secured on favourable terms the lease of the site adjoining the tramway power station and this included a foundry, so they were able to get cheap castings. Gratings were made in the foundry and delivered over Somerset and Wiltshire on the backs of their buses. The foundry was used for war work and brought in a 'handsome revenue'.

In about 1909–10 the registered office of the Bath company in London was moved from 18 St Helen's Place to 119–125 Finsbury Pavement, EC, also Sir Vincent Caillard was replaced as a Director by E. Caillard, who now left the Sunderland Board. Sir Vincent later became a Director of Vickers Ltd and the Metropolitan–Vickers Electrical Co. Ltd, as well as Beyer-Peacock and the London Chatham & Dover Railway. In about 1916 E. Caillard was replaced as a Director by J.B. Hamilton, General Manager of Leeds City Tramways, who had recently reported on the Bath system. Sir James Sivewright, after being Chairman for a few years until Hamilton took over, resigned and went to live at Kincardine in Scotland.

As no dividend had been declared since 1906, at the general meeting on 4th June, 1914 a committee was appointed by shareholders to confer with the Board on the management of finances. The committee sought the help of Balfour, Beatty & Co. Ltd, the tramway experts, and their report quite confirmed the very unfavourable opinion that the committee had formed of the management of the undertaking. 'The energies of the Company were being frittered away in a foundry which cost only a few hundred pounds, but the profits of which were said to amount to 15–20 per cent.' The report said that the bus sideline had not furnished any revenue and the whole undertaking was very much overstaffed. A member of the committee, attacking the Board said, 'Money had been invested in tea shops and side-shows, which apparently took up so much time of the manager that the tramways had been neglected'.

The Board was so dissatisfied with Balfour's report that, as mentioned above it asked J.B. Hamilton to make an assessment. He found that the undertaking was being maintained in a state of the highest productive capacity by the tramway manager and his staff, and that work was being most economically carried out, reflecting the utmost credit on all concerned. In fact Hamilton was so impressed by the BET that he invested in the undertaking and became 'a fairly large shareholder'.

War brought its problems: in March 1916 W.E. Hardy, the general manager, asked for the retention of a stoker from the forces as there were only three stokers left, and one was required for each shift. On 14th April, 1916 trams had their lights subdued; a mask was fitted to the headlights and the lights in the destination boxes were extinguished (the latter lights were restored on 26th April) and the inside curtains drawn. In the gloom upstairs, some passengers tried to get rid of foreign or doubtful coins. The same month, Sivewright announced that 171 BET men had joined the services and fifty of them had attested and worn armlets, making 221 attached to the

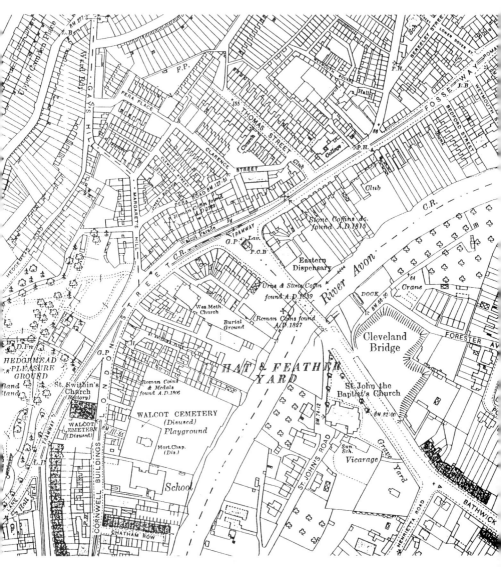

NORTH OF THE CITY CENTRE

This series of reduced size maps have been reproduced and reduced from the 1932, 25″ Ordnance Survey maps.

THE CITY CENTRE

OLD BRIDGE AND GREAT
WESTERN RAILWAY STATION

THE 'GREEN TREE' AND WELLS ROAD

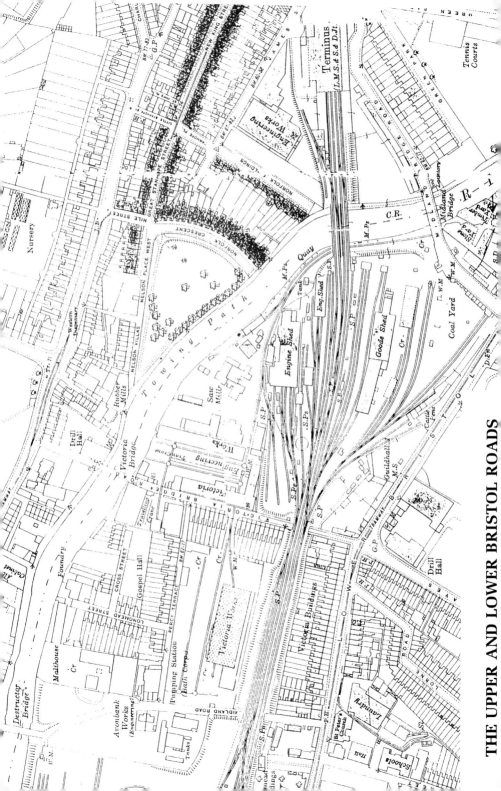

THE UPPER AND LOWER BRISTOL ROADS

THE LOWER BRISTOL ROAD AND HERBERT ROAD

forces. Conductresses started in October 1915 and a special seat was made for them at the foot of the stairs. They turned the trolley round, but to avoid having them run to the front with the point bar, in December 1915 drivers were issued with long point bars so that they could lean over the dash and do it themselves. In September 1916 women started to learn tram driving. They mostly worked on the Twerton and Weston roads and only went on the hillier route to Combe Down if there were no men available.

In 1917 the BET carried 27,000 wounded soldiers stationed at the convalescent hospital, Combe Park, free of charge. The company could not continue to bear this expense and from the beginning of 1918, fares were paid by a fund started by the *Bath Chronicle*.

Power costs rose by nearly £500 and a 'steam saving arrangement' was adopted. The government asked for a voluntary 15 per cent reduction of fuel. J.B. Hamilton, by now the company's Chairman, became a member of the Board of Trade National Tramways Committee set up by the government to control tramway undertakings. W.E. Hardy was employed on important government work — for which he was given the MBE — in connection with control of mines, being employed on the technical side as to the use of coal for steam raising.

As mentioned earlier, the Company's 1901 Light Railway Order took the Twerton route only as far as Twerton GWR station, but six months later, at the request of Bath Corporation, an 18-chain extension was added, which was authorised, and in due course constructed in 1903. After 1908 this extension was only used by workers cars, most trams going only as far as the station.

From January 1918 onwards this length became completely disused, all trams terminating at the station. It was not actually abandoned, however, and still remained *in situ* although not used, and the official total route length, of 14.78 miles in the early days, remained the same right up until 1938.

To assist fare collection, books of a dozen 1*d*. or 1½*d*. tickets were sold for 1*s*. and 1*s*.6*d*. respectively; later 2½*d*. and 3½*d*. books were sold. At the end of the War, of the 282 men employed by the BET in August 1914, 182 joined up and altogether 240 left to enlist (some who replaced those who had enlisted, joined up themselves later); 18 were killed on service. As drivers became demobilised, men taken on as drivers during the War were given the option of conducting or leaving when the former drivers returned. By mid-March 1919, nearly a score of conductresses had been replaced by men.

Owing to the dissatisfaction with the latest award of the Government Committee on Production, which gave male employees of certain tram and bus companies that were bound by the committee's award a 5*s*. war bonus to meet the increased cost of living, and did not increase the women's wage, the London & Provincial Licensed Vehicle Workers' Union members were called out. All Bath trams were off the road by 5 pm on 19th August, 1918.

Hitherto, the BET had run a special car at 5.18 every afternoon from the GWR station to the War Hospital, Combe Park. On the 19th there was a large crowd of cripples at Kingsmead Square. The office staff and employees conferred, and two special cars left the depot, but on arrival at Kingsmead Square, they found that some of the more able-bodied had walked on and others had been given lifts and only one car was actually used.

A car was used later in the evening to carry passengers from the City to the Frome bus at the Glasshouse, as it was felt that country people brought to the City should not be stranded. It was driven by an inspector with a lady inspector acting as a conductress. Only bus passengers were allowed to use it. Few people had expected the sudden strike — not even the employees. Relations with the office were happy; it was a national, not local, strike.

Absence of trams affected delivery of goods which were being increasingly carried by tram in this period of transport shortage. Trams were used to convey bags of mail to outlying districts, and postmen used them to start their rounds. The terms under dispute were promised to be settled and an award given, and Bath trams resumed on 23rd August.

In 1920 capital was needed to buy more buses, but people could not be induced to invest in BET as no dividend had been paid since 1906, and so a subsidiary company was formed to take over the buses. The new company, 'Bath Tramways Motor Co. Ltd.', was formed on 30th July, 1920, to take over the motor business and foundry as from 1st January, 1920. J.B. Hamilton, the BET Chairman, was also Chairman of the BTM Co. The BET was paid for the buses £19,935 in cash and £20,000 in shares of the BTM. Two other long-standing BET Directors, E.H.R. Trenow and H.F. Clutterbuck, also became BTM Directors. Most of the buses were purchased from AEC, and as early as Easter 1926 almost all of them were on pneumatic tyres.

Trams stopped running during the General Strike in 1926 and, on 4th May FB 05, an A.E.C. single-decker bus, ran a service in lieu of trams from Devonshire Buildings to Lambridge, and carried 700 passengers that day. Hardy threatened pickets who tried to stop the bus coming out that they would be charged with attempted suicide. The strike breakers had dodged pickets by crossing the river by boat and getting in the back way. Then Hardy issued a special notice: 'Following the notice posted yesterday, we now announce that we are going to call in outside aid. Any man not reporting for work by twelve noon tomorrow, May 8th, will no longer be guaranteed his job'. This brought most of the men back, but Hardy only took them on condition that they signed saying they would not join a trade union. Thirty-two men were not re-engaged after the strike as they refused to sign such a form. The tram service re-started on 10th May. During the strike, the small engine in the power house had been kept running by the office staff, as it supplied electricity to the foundry which was not on strike.

By 1930 E.H.R. Trenow was now Chairman and Managing Director of the BET, and the other three Directors were Colonel H.F. Clutterbuck, Major the Hon. Eric Long, and John Aimé Roney; H.J. Almond was still the Secretary. The same five held the same positions in the BTM also. In addition Trenow was now Chairman, and Roney a Director and Secretary, of the Ceara Tramway Light & Power Co. Ltd in Brazil, which had only these two as Directors.

In 1932 the Lavington & Devizes Motor Services Ltd, an old-established and quite large independent rural bus operator dating back to 1912, was purchased by the BTM, but retained as a separate subsidiary company and not absorbed, although all its Directors resigned and were replaced by Trenow, Clutterbuck, Roney and Long.

The L&D had about 13 buses and six coaches working 15 routes in the Chippenham-Devizes-Pewsey-Andover-Salisbury-Frome-Trowbridge   area to the south-east of Bath, as compared with about 80 buses and coaches of the BTM itself working 25 routes, mostly country ones, but including also about 10 locals in the city area.

Under the Light Railway Order of 1901 the Corporation of the City of Bath had the right to compulsorily purchase the Bath Electric Tramways within six months after 32 years from the date when the Board of Trade certified the railway, or any part of it, to be fit for traffic, and the value was to be determined under Section 43 of the Tramways Act of 1870. This was by paying the value of the tramway at the time of purchase, and of all its lands, buildings, works, and materials, but exclusive of any allowance for past or future profits, or any compensation for compulsory sale, or other consideration. The Bath purchase date was fixed at 13th January, 1936. Bath Corporation promoted a Parliamentary Bill in the 1936 Session, a comprehensive affair seeking powers for sundry other items as well. Part V, dealing with Road Transport, Clause 27, asked that within 12 months after the passing of this Act, the Corporation could give to the Bath Electric Tramways Limited and the Bath Tramways Motor Co. Ltd notice of its intention to purchase both undertakings. Clause 35 provided for the winding up of the Tramway Company after the transfer, and Clause 38 asked for all its powers, rights, privileges and authorities under the Light Railway Orders of 1901 to 1909 to be transferred to and vested in the Corporation. Clause 40 was to empower the Corporation to maintain, but not manufacture, and to run motor buses along all the tram routes. Clause 42 was to authorise the Corporation after the date of the transfer to abandon and discontinue the tramways.

However, all items referring to the tramways were later deleted from this Bill, and when the Bath Corporation Act of 1937 (1 Edw.8,cap.cxvii) received the Royal Assent on 30th July, 1937, there was no mention of tramways, and the Act dealt mainly with the Hospital for Rheumatic Diseases, buildings of historic or architectural interest, the sale of coal and coke, staff superannuation, financial matters, libraries, gas, and water. The Act's 67 pages also gave the Corporation powers to widen seven streets, viz Northgate Street, Walcot Street, Avon Street, Corn Street, Milk Street, Barton Street, and The Ambury. Of these, only the first two were used by the tramways.

In December 1936 another purchaser arrived. The Bristol Tramways & Carriage Co. Ltd, whose direct predecessor had owned the original Bath horse tramways in 1880, purchased 96 per cent of the issued share capital of Bath Electric Tramways Limited, keeping it as a separate subsidiary. Trenow, Clutterbuck, Roney, and Long all remained as Directors of both BET and BTM, but were immediately joined by John Frederick Heaton as Chairman, and Major Francis J. Chapple, making a total of six. Chapple had for many years been General Manager of the Bristol company, whilst Heaton was Chairman and Managing Director of Thomas Tilling Limited, half-owner of the National Omnibus, which jointly owned Western National, and which, since December 1931, half-owned the Bristol company. The BET and BTM registered offices were immediately transferred from 119–125 Finsbury Pavement, London, to 1–3 St Augustine's Place, Bristol, and H.J. Almond was replaced as Secretary by E.G. Kingston. At the same time E.H.R. Trenow, the long-serving Bath Managing Director, also became a Director of the Bristol company. The Lavington company was wound up in 1937 and absorbed by BTM, which owned 92 buses by 1940.

When BTCC took BET over in 1936, the equipment was becoming life-expired. It had been very well maintained, but the new owners decided to abolish trams and replace them with buses. The announcement of the change-over was made by Alderman A.W. Wills at a meeting of the City Council on 27th July, 1937, the day after he had concluded the agreement with the Bristol Tramways & Carriage Co. Ltd.

The first section to be abandoned was Newbridge Road–Newton St Loe, which was closed on 29th October, 1938. Twerton cars finished on 22nd April, 1939 and gave drivers a chance to get used to driving double-decker buses on a flat route. Country bus drivers took over the running of the double-deckers at first, while the ex-tram drivers drove the single-deck country buses. The rest of the City routes were withdrawn on 6th May; 16 cars coming out of service during the day were driven to a scrapyard consisting of two sidings which had been laid down at Midford Road opposite St Martin's Hospital (formerly the Workhouse), while the trams used during the late evening were scrapped at the depot, No. 22, the last tram to Combe Down, already had a full load of passengers making a round trip and when it had nearly reached the terminus inspector Smale ordered the conductor to run round with the trolley before it reached the automatic reverser, and the tram started off on its return journey before the waiting crowd knew what was happening. No. 22 was the last tram from the Guildhall to the Depot and was 'driven' by the mayor, Captain Adrian Hopkins, assisted by inspector Smale (who had his hand on the controller) and inspector Hale working the handbrake. On arrival at the depot, Hopkins switched off the generator engines, which had been running for 35 years. 'As these slowed down and came to rest, there was a silence which nobody attempted to break.' The party adjourned to the company's offices at No. 10 Northgate Street, where they drank sherry.

Fittings and glass from the trams had been booked and sold a month before scrapping. Seats were sold at 3s., 2s. and 1s., while plate glass windows fetched 2s. 6d. a sheet. The trolley booms became wireless aerials, while the rods which held the strap hangers were used as staircase hand-rails. Some lengths of lifted rail were bent at an angle, and soon after the start of the 1939 war they were put at the entrances to the city so that they could be placed in holes in the road to form a block in case of invasion.

The 34 double-deck and six single-deck trams were replaced by buses: 30

double-deck and 10 new single-deckers. Fourteen double-deckers were completely new, but the other 16 were on second-hand chassis built in 1936, 12 for Maidstone & District Motor Services Ltd and four for its subsidiary the Chatham & District Traction Company. All 40 were on Bristol chassis with new bodies built by Bristol at their Body Building Works at Brislington. These vehicles were owned and operated by Bath Electric Tramways Ltd, which continued to exist separately from the Bath Tramways Motor Co. Ltd. An increased population due to evacuation of the Admiralty to Bath caused Bath Electric Tramways Ltd in January 1941 to augment its fleet with six 1931 A.E.C. Regent open-staircase double-deckers hired from Brighton Hove & District Omnibus Co. Ltd, which were replaced in December 1942 by six enclosed-staircase Regents of 1930 on hire from London Transport, all these remaining at Bath until February 1946, but no new buses were available until the spring of 1947, when two new Bristol double-deckers arrived, followed later the same year by some transferred from the Bristol operating fleet.

Hence by 1942 BET buses were working 20 local routes, some of them linked in cross-city pairs, of which six were ex-tram, two were new, and 12 had been worked before the war by BTM. The BET buses never operated from the Walcot Street tram depot, and right from the start in 1939 they were all garaged at the old-established BTM premises in London Road, Kensington, which over the years have been greatly enlarged. Although the original garage nearer the main road was demolished and replaced in 1961–62 by a new garage and overhaul works further back and parallel to the River Avon, nevertheless the open storage area today is large. The original buildings in Walcot Street of both the tram depot and the power station still stand today hardly altered at all, apart from the gutting of their interiors and both are now in use as a parking or storage garage for private motor cars, with a thriving Antiques Sales Market in the tram depot every Saturday.

As Director of both the BET and BTM companies, Trenow (who had been a Director for almost 40 years and Chairman and Managing Director for much of this time) stayed only until 1940. Clutterbuck (who had been a BET Director for almost 50 years), Roney and Long, all retained their Directorships until 1950, Major the Hon. Eric Long becoming a Viscount in the mid-1940s. For over 30 years after tramway abandonment the BET fleet remained fairly constant at around 40 buses, and the BTM fleet fell gradually from about 120 to approximately 105 (with far more double-deckers than in earlier times), until both companies were finally absorbed into the Bristol Omnibus Co. Ltd on 1st January, 1970. In 1983 the Bristol company split itself geographically into two, and on 1st January, 1986 the southern half was re-named Badgerline Limited, with its registered offices at Weston-super-Mare. This now operates most of the local services at Bath, both City and Country, although there are also several small independent operators. The local administrative (as distinct from registered) offices had remained in the old tramway offices at 10, Northgate Street until March 1958 when they were transferred to the new Bath bus station between Dorchester Street and Railway Street which was opened that month.

Today, almost the whole of the centre of the City is still not altered too much from the tramway period. One can still walk the streets of Bath, some of them quite narrow, and visualise electric tramways as they were 50 to 85 years ago, and understand why the passing loops were put where they were. Five of the ex-tram routes have been extended further outwards, but otherwise buses still mainly follow the tram routes. Southgate Street has been pedestrianized and buses now use Manvers Street and Pierrepont Street in both directions. Broad Street and The Paragon, although still open, are now not used by buses following ex-tram routes and these now use Walcot Street and Ladymead in both directions. The Combe Down route has been cut short at Foxhill, Combe Down itself being reached by a separate and more direct route.

The Foxhill and Bathford routes are now worked by double-deck buses, Twerton and Upper Weston by full-size single-deckers, Oldfield Park by minibuses, and Newton St Loe by double-deckers *en route* to Bristol.. All the 14 other City routes are now worked by minibuses, except Odd Down, which has full-size single-deckers (and was a proposed tram route in 1899). The Old Bridge over the River Avon was demolished in 1966, and replaced by Churchill Bridge a short distance downstream, one-way traffic schemes being introduced north and south of the river. A new housing estate has been built on the lower part of the proposed Lansdown rack railway, but all the rest of its route is still unspoilt open green fields or downland.

One bus, a Bristol VR double-decker, was repainted in 1989 in light blue and cream tramway livery instead of the normal green and yellow of the other buses. Prominently displayed on both sides and ends was the legend '1904 Bath Electric Tramways 1989' in proper shaded tramway style of lettering, to mark the fiftieth anniversary of abandonment. This vehicle worked regularly on the Bathford to Foxhill ex-tramway service, and several of the country routes.

BATH ELECTRIC TRAMWAYS Ltd.

OFFICIAL

TRAM & OMNIBUS TIME TABLE & GUIDE

BATH TRAMWAYS MOTOR Co. Ltd.

№ 2521   DECEMBER 193?

PRICE ONE PENNY.

SPEAR'S BATH

Sausages

and

First Prize Wiltshire Bacon

As supplied to their Trade Customers throughout the country.

Bath Electric Tramways Milnes-Daimler bus outside the District Council Offices, Midsomer Norton, *c.*1907. Note the parcel box on the canopy.   *Author's Collection*

Car 26 at the Bathford terminus. The blind has been changed to indicate 'Glasshouse', but not all the outside seats have been reversed ready for the return journey. The rope is wrapped round the trolley pole which was standard practice at Bath; the trolley will be turned by the automatic reverser. Advertisements on the window of the lower deck publicise: Rugby – Bath v Portsmouth (left-hand window); Green Motor Coach Tours (centre window); Bath City v Clandown and Yeovil; the Glasshouse Cafe (right-hand window). View *c.*1935.   *Dr H.A. Whitcombe*

Chapter Four

Rolling Stock

At the opening there were 18 double-deck cars (Nos. 1 to 18) and two single-deck (Nos. 50 & 51) combination cars, all of Milnes construction, the latter with typical Milnes plain arch-top windows; by February another eight double-deck and two single-deck cars were delivered, and also one combined watering car and track cleaner. The double-deck cars were 27 ft 8 in. in length and 6 ft 9 in. wide, while the single-deckers were 28 ft long and 6 ft 6 in. wide. The trucks were made by W.C.F. Busch, Bautzen, Saxony, and were simple, robust structures with one-piece sills in solid forged steel of channel section, with semi-elliptical springs at each end to support the car body and reduce pitching. They had a 6 ft wheelbase.

A Milnes lifeguard was fitted at each end of the cars, the tray being lifted by a lever under the stairs, usually operated by being jumped on as it was heavy to work. The stairways were the ordinary pattern and cars had extended canopies. The swivel head trolleys with graphite brushes were made by Brecknell, Munro & Rogers.

Each car had two Westinghouse 49B-type 30 hp motors and 90M controllers, and a British Westinghouse patent (Newell) magnetic brake in addition to the handbrake. Later an automatic sand valve was fitted which dropped sand when the magnetic brake was applied hard, and when this occurred, the driver was required to knock the sand off the track, to avoid causing a derailment. Also at some later date, the handbrake was altered to the Peacock quick acting pattern. At first there were seven power and five brake notches, but this was altered to eight power and seven brake notches. Car No. 5 was speeded up about 1923 by W.J. Coward & Co., Bath, who fitted higher gearing and roller bearings. Some other cars, including Nos. 17, 26 and 32 were altered, but the load on the power station was reputed to be too great, and all were converted back to normal except No. 5 which was very popular with motormen as it made their work easier. One said: 'No. 5 had a speed and a half of the others'. The best pulling cars ran on the hilly Combe Down route, the worst on the flat Twerton road. The first notch of the magnetic brake on the speeded-up trams was not functional.

Ten more cars were delivered in 1904, certainly by August, and these had minor differences from the original batch. Nos. 27–34 had no upper deck lights on standards at the head of the stairs and relied solely on light coming through the rear of the destination boxes. These cars had extra stanchions supporting the canopy from the offside of the dash. Most of the earlier cars were modified to have this feature in later years, but it was slightly different as it joined the dash by means of a curve. The brass rail from the platform step to the canopy on the later cars was close to the riser, instead of on the outside, and this prevented large prams being loaded on platforms of Nos. 27–34.

Single-deck cars Nos. 54 and 55 had narrower steps and an extra one, and a well for the driver to stand in. The first four cars were known as 'high steppers' and the last two as 'low steppers', passengers preferring the easier access of the latter. Drivers preferred them too as the narrower steps were less likely to be scraped squeezing through a narrow gap. The dashes were a

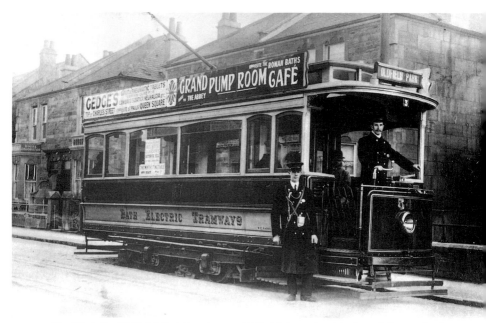

No. 54 at the Oldfield Park terminus, c.1909. Note route plate 3, and the conductor with a Bell Punch as opposed to a 'Williamson'; motorman George Dick, conductor Jack Eglington.   *Author's Collection*

No. 52 in the Lower Bristol Road *en route* to Oldfield Park, 1939. Driven by motorman Humphries, conductor Hunt and inspector Gallop stand on the rear platform.
                                                                                S. Miles Davey

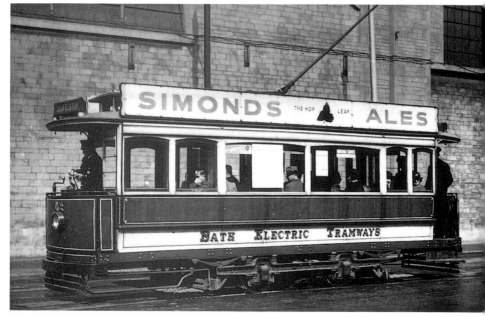

different shape and the controllers were central instead of off-set. One driver whose shoulder was wounded in the War was unable to reach both the controller and the handbrake of Nos. 50–53 and had to change cars with someone who was driving No. 54 or 55. At first the single-deckers had ropes to turn the trolleys, but within a year, a bamboo cane carried on a rack on the side of the truck was substituted. This may have been the result of a passenger on the top deck of a Twerton car on 27th February, 1904, being lassoed by the rope of a passing combination car, dragging him off on to the road!

The inside seats of all cars were upholstered with dark blue cloth relieved with a red pattern, but about 1924 were replaced by more hygienic cane seats, and 10 years later, these in turn were replaced by slat seats. Twenty-two persons could be seated inside. The 33 upstairs seats had waterproof covers fastened with two lugs and eyelets and conductors had to check that they were neatly folded between seat and rail. They were usually flung down on the floor by passengers, and were abolished about 1925 as their condition deteriorated; and so on a crowded tram, men stood upstairs in the rain when the seats were too wet to sit on. On one side there were six reversible double seats and a single reversible seat by the trolley standard; while there were seven double seats on the other side. There was a seat for three passengers over each canopy.

The single-deck cars, colloquially known as 'whippets', carried 30 passengers, seating 16 passengers inside and seven outside at each end, with all seats longitudinal, 3+8+4 on each side. The Board of Trade created a fuss about passengers at the front of these cars not being separated from the driver. These combination cars were mainly used for the Oldfield Park route, but did appear on other roads, particularly Twerton on Sunday mornings, and also at holiday times when double-deck cars were taken off and given to the Combe Down and Bathford service.

Destination boxes on the double-deck cars were lowered about 1905 as their height caused them to be struck and damaged when the trolley pole was turned. At first a conductor had to remember to bring his brass key to turn the destination linens — if he left it at home, he had to take the cover off the box to turn it, but about 1910 fixed handles were fitted. No. 21 had side destination rolls fitted to the centre windows in the 1920s. In the early days a few cars had holders for wooden destination boards above the decency boards instead of just below the windows as became standard practice. Above the driver on the edge of the canopy was painted 'Swing the pole this side →', but this was removed by 1908 as the electrical wiring had been modified to allow the boom to swing through 360 degrees. Above the bulkhead window was a red/green light, electric bell and conductor's bell push. About 1919 the conductor's bell was modified to a mechanical pull strap bell, as conductors had to 'ring off' trams while facing the rear, and with an electric bell push above the bulkhead window this was a physically difficult procedure. No. 17 was the first car so altered. Blue curtains were originally fitted to shield passengers from the sun and were used for blackout during the War, but were abolished soon afterwards.

No. 54 at the Oldfield Park terminus in Cynthia Road, 18th April, 1938. This car has a rounded dash and central controller.   *W.A. Camwell*

Cars at Odd Down scrapyard in May 1939. No. 53 is on the right. This car has a flatter dash than No. 54.   *S. Miles Davey*

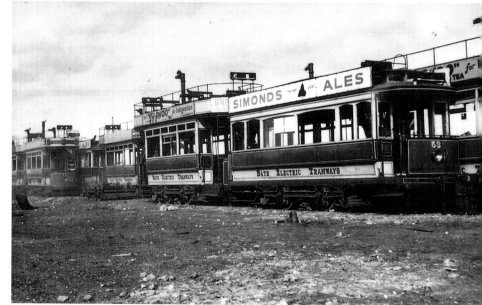

Power meters to check consumption of electricity by each driver were fitted, but taken off about 1920. Motormen who drifted a lot and cut their power consumption had their names on the Good Conduct board. About 1928, the carpenter made an experimental screen in front of the driver on single-deck car No. 54. Trouble was experienced at night with reflections on the glass, also from rain drops, as no wiper was fitted, and it brought an unpleasant draught across the motorman's back. It necessarily protruded beyond the fender to give clearance to the handbrake, and if adopted would have required an expensive alteration of the fender. The screen was removed after about a week. A similar experiment was made on double-deck car No. 26 about 1917, which had a zinc shield hanging from the canopy to the level of the driver's eyes, but this was not satisfactory and was removed.

About 1929 windows were put up at the end of the open seats on the combination cars to protect passengers from the wind. These open ends outside the double doors were used by smokers. Wooden ticket boxes for used tickets were fitted about 1931, below the bulkhead window on double-deck cars and on the inside of the dash on the combination cars. They were made by the company's carpenter and the mahogany was magnificent. Conductors had to keep the floor clear of dead tickets. They picked them up, tore them in half and before the introduction of the boxes, threw them into the road. If they were rushed and there were no passengers inside, they opened the doors about 200 yds from a terminus and let the draught blow them out. If an inspector saw a ticket on the floor he was likely to say, 'You got a bad back?'

Sixteen bags of sand were kept under the seats in groups of four and there was also an emergency sand box under the stairs. Equipment included a duster and handbrush so the conductor could clean the car.

Double-deck cars had advertisements on the decency boards, small hopper windows and shades on interior lamps. The combination cars had advertisements on the lamp shades, while roof advertisement boards were fitted February 1909. Bills were posted on the windows of both types of tram, with Bath Tramways Torpedo Car notices taking pride of place in the centre window. Passengers disliked these window bills as they obscured the view.

Each of the cars had a different character: No. 20 was slow, and No. 23 a terrible puller and called 'Sleepy Lizzie'. No. 50 was a fast car. No. 10 was a special car as it could be converted for use as a rail grinder, being adapted by Brecknell, Munro & Rogers Ltd in 1912. The brake handle had a large wheel below it, so the carborundum block which replaced the magnetic brake when grinding corrugations out of the rails, could be screwed down hard on the rail. The handle operated the ordinary hand brake while the wheel screwed down the carborundum block. There were two spindles one inside the other, grinding gear spindle outermost. Drivers, especially the short ones, hated No. 10 as the wheel made the brake handle less accessible and stiffer to operate. Also a driver's watch chain often caught in the brake handle when he leant forward to alter the points. When grinding, No. 10 carried four large barrels of water inside for cooling the carborundum blocks, the water being led through rubber tubes and controlled by cocks. If

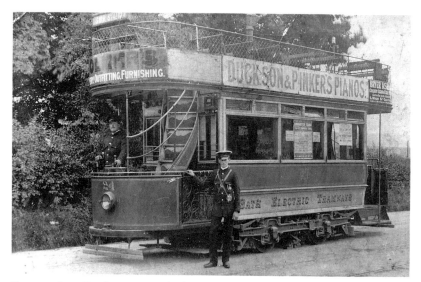

Car 24 at Cross Roads Loop, Newbridge Road, c.1911. The power meter is to the right of the stairs; the conductor's bell to the left; route plate 7 can be seen by the top of the stanchion. Later No. 24 had another stanchion to support the canopy added on the far side of the driver. Motorman Bill Lane and conductor Percy Jell are on the wrong line, as they are probably waiting for a car to come from Newton on the nearer track before eventually following it to the GWR station.   *Author's Collection*

No. 10 which doubled as a rail grinder, at the Combe Down terminus, c.1912. As it is crewed by works staff and the curtains are drawn, it is probably on grinding duty. If so, the magnetic brake shoe will have been replaced by a carborundum block and there will be tanks of water inside to cool the rail. The wheel outside the brake handle was used for screwing down the carborundum block. BET monogram on side of car.
                    T. Streicher Collection

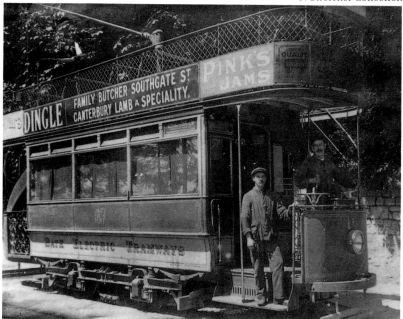

No. 14 at the Weston Hotel *en route* for Weston, 10th September, 1937. The board in the centre window reads: 'To and From the Royal United Hospital'. This hospital had been moved in May 1933 from the city centre to a site in Combe Park adjacent to Bath War Hospital. *H.B. Priestley*

No. 13 at The Crown Inn, Bathford, the destination blind reading 'Devonshire Arms' – in later years this became 'Devonshire Bdgs' (buildings). Photographed in 1915, the tram is crewed by motorman W.G. Swift and conductor Adams. *Author's Collection*

Car 27 at the GWR station, *c*.1908. Note the high destination boxes, and the only lights upstairs are on the rear of the boxes; BET monogram on the side panel. Motorman Poole and conductor Gallop are the crew. *Author's Collection*

Motorman Jack Snow with car 16 on full power climbing across the New Bridge, 18th April, 1938. Current is fed to the overhead at the pole in the background. The field behind No. 16 is now used for the Newbridge Park & Ride bus service. *W.A. Camwell*

Nos. 21 and 2 near the top of Wellsway, c.1904. The route board above the advertisement was later lowered to the window sills. The notice on the end of the canopy reads: 'Swing the pole this side → '. Inspectors Hale and McConnochie, driver Callan and conductor Poole are in view. *Author's Collection*

In December 1895, No. 18 waits at Lambridge prior to setting out for the Devonshire Arms with motorman W.G. Swift and conductress Cashnella. Note that the headlamp is partly shaded. *Author's Collection*

going to Oldfield Park for grinding, the trolley standard was taken off, and a single-deck boom put on which was without a standard; the destination boxes and lights were removed so that it was able to go under the Green Tree arch. This conversion took about four hours. Men on spare duty took No. 10 out for a couple of hours grinding. When not grinding, No. 10 was used on the Weston and Newton roads and usually had smaller diameter wheels.

About six cars had provision on the chassis for track cleaners to be fitted — knives which could be screwed down by hand. One knife went down into the groove while the other cleaned the running surface. When fitted, a car had four sets of knives.

Water Car and Decorated Cars

The existence of a water car was mentioned in the descriptions of the system in various journals in February 1904, though in June we read of McCarter answering Bath R.D.C.'s letter of complaint on the state of the roads, saying that he hoped to have the sprinkler ready for use in a few days. Hearing this a councillor remarked: 'They have it now and they had an accident with it. It has been in our district and looked like a torpedo boat destroyer; it was about twice the size of a tram and painted black'. Another councillor said that he had seen it in a ditch in the Wells Road. As Milnes did not build works' cars, the truck, and Westinghouse motors and controllers were supplied, and the rest of the car built, by Brecknell, Munro & Rogers Ltd at Bristol.

The water car sprayed the road on a hot day to cool it and prevent tar running on the rails and causing slipping on hills. On untarred roads it laid the dust to prevent it getting in the rails and slowing the cars down. Between the platforms was a large tank with a trolley boom on top. The car was usually driven by depot staff and only two men were authorised to drive it — care was needed as the water flopped about and caused it to sway badly. It was fitted with a brush at each end set at an angle for cleaning the rails, and snow clearance, turned by an electric motor on the driver's platform, which was at a higher level than on the passenger cars. The brush was raised and lowered by turning a wheel. The car was kept at the bottom of No. 8 road in the depot and was known as 'Black Maria'.

In 1909 when the Bath Pageant was held, No. 32 was decorated and toured the city and during the day was parked on a disused line at the Guildhall as a booking office for bus excursions. In 1923 a tram and charabanc were decorated, illuminated and toured the city to collect for the Mayor's Distress Fund for the unemployed. The switch kept blowing on this car, so alterations had to be made. The tram ran in March 1923 and collected £230 in 10 days.

Livery

The cars were kept in superb condition and painted every 2½ years. A chargehand and two mates painted the cars on No. 1 road behind tarpaulins to keep the dust away. A double-deck car took just over a fortnight and a combination car a little less. The painters mixed their own colours at the depot. First a grey undercoat was put on, then grey filler which was faced down with soda brick and knifing filler put in the cracks. This was faced down with wet and dry paper, then a grey coat and blue undercoat applied with a camel hair brush 3 inches wide or less. Then, blue enamel was put on which was faced down with pumice powder to an egg shell finish. The pumice powder was applied with pads made from motormen's old serge coats cut into 4 inch squares. Then a coat of hard-drying varnish was applied and after a light flannelling with pumice powder, the finishing coat of varnish was put on. Transfer numbers gold shaded with red were applied to the dash.

If the upstairs floor was in bad condition, it was stripped, red oxide applied, then a layer of canvas with lead paint to seal it and wood battens nailed on top. It was then tarred. Netting was light grey, almost aluminium, with the top rail and stair rails maroon. Destination boxes were painted lead, then black, lined at the back with white. Trucks were maroon with black springs. The lifeguard gate was black.

Inside, the roof was of varnished maple wood. All varnish work was flattened with pumice powder and this had to be carefully washed off or the finished job would have been made 'lousy' with bits.

Medium blue. Cant rail, waist panel, dash and stair bands, lined white. Platform step and trolley mast. Until about 1920 cars had gold BET monogram on waist panel.

Primrose yellow. Upper deck panelling, window frames, rocker panel and bulkhead. Black outer line and blue inner line on rocker panel. Title on rocker panel in gold shaded blue. Upper deck panels lined blue only. Stair risers yellow and black.

White. Inside of dash. Controller black.

Maroon. Truck, lifeguard tray, handrails and iron scrollwork at corner of dash.

Selection of 2½d. and 3d. tickets from the collection of J.J. Luckman.

Laying the Southgate Street/Dorchester Street curve on 14th August, 1903. The Old Bridge is to the right.

Author's Collection

The road near Walcot Church closed to vehicular traffic for track laying in 1903. During this period traffic was diverted via Cleveland Toll Bridge, which was temporarily freed of tolls.

Author's Collection

Chapter Five

The Permanent Way and Electrical Equipment

The total route length remained constant at 14 m. 62 ch. (14.78 miles) from 1908 until 1939. Official statistics were quoted in miles and chains until 1923 and in miles and decimals of a mile from 1924 onwards. The length of double track fell from 4 m. 46 ch. to 4 m. 20 ch., and then to 3 m. 72 ch. by 1926, at which figure (3.90 miles) it then remained constant. At the same time the length of single track rose from 10 m. 15 ch. to 10 m. 36 ch., and then to 10 m. 70 ch., and then remained constant at 10.88 miles. This was because Bath started off with too many passing loops, and some were removed in due course. The total track mileage thus fell from 19 m. 28 ch. to 19 m. 02 ch. and then to 18 m. 54 ch. (18.68 miles). Although the outer end of the Twerton route was disused after 1918 it does not appear to have been legally abandoned, as the official statistics do not appear to show any reduction. The official track mileage remained at 18.68 right to the end, but the effective track mileage appears to have been 18.25 if allowing for the non-use of the Twerton extension and also several passing loops which fell into disuse latterly. Adding 0.32 miles for the depot and sidings gives a grand total of 19.00 track miles.

Rails were in 45 ft lengths weighing 95 lb./yd and bedded on six inches of concrete, though 300 yds of double track in Lower Borough Walls by the Royal United Hospital, was laid on 8 in. by 4 in. timber sleepers for quietness. The rails were supplied by the North Eastern Steel Co. The worst curves had manganese steel rails on both sides. The points were mainly of Hadfield's patent 'Era' manganese steel, though some were supplied by Lorain Steel Co. Loops had the usual automatic switch for the correct road. Wood paving was laid between the track in the centre of the City and granite setts and macadam in the outskirts. About 20 men were employed on permanent way maintenance; their materials were carried round in a cart drawn by a horse, but sometimes pulled by a tram. Spare rails were kept at the foundry, and the tar boiler, fish plates and small items kept at the Company's yard in Dog Street. A subsidiary yard was located near the Trinity Brewery, Kingsmead Square; and until 1920, the Porter Butt Hotel yard was used as well.

From 1904 to about 1920 a London firm joined the butt ends of the rails by thermit welding; the company in 1917 used electric arc welding for minor repairs which they did themselves, getting power from the overhead by a long pole. An oxy-acetylene flame was used for cutting and drilling the rails and also to harden the rail *in situ* to prolong its life. W.E. Hardy, the manager, was one of the leading authorities in the country on cutting, hardening and welding tram rails. In 1915 Hardy pioneered by laying in the Lower Bristol Road the first tarmacadam against a tram track in the country, and did so against world opinion. Engineers came from all parts to see it, and found it a success. Hardy gave a Conference Paper in 1924 describing how he had replaced wood blocks with tarmacadam, which he found excellent for light road traffic but not so good for heavy steel-tyred drays. In 1926 two miles of track were relaid, with all the joints welded, some by the Thermit process and some electrically.

No. 3 engine in the power house, 21st February, 1904. The governor's weights can be seen above the crosshead. At the top of the picture is a 16 ton crane built at Bath by Stothert & Pitt Limited in 1903.   *Author's Collection*

The superheater tubes can be seen below No. 3 boiler being installed in the power house on 1st October, 1903.   *Author's Collection*

Two men were employed to clean the points: one on the Combe Down–Bathford road and the other on Twerton and Newton. The pointsmen rode round with brine to free the points in cold weather and it was not unknown for a driver to go into a house to ask for water to unfreeze a point. The automatic points were all right in cold weather, but the hand-operated ones were sometimes difficult to shift. A special pointsman operated the points and overhead at the Old Bridge until about 1928.

The steepest gradient on the whole system was 1-in-9, and the sharpest curve was of 36 ft radius. The Wells Road route climbed steadily for nearly two miles all the way from Old Bridge to the Glasshouse, rising 450 ft in that distance. All routes were single track with loops, and some loops were longer than the minimum, but the only substantial section of double track was for half a mile mainly up the steep hill in Wells Road from near the bottom as far as Kipling Avenue. The Oldfield Park, Bathford, and Newton termini originally had a double-track layout, but the second track was later removed in each case, and Bath became notable for the long stretch of single line with which all six routes ended.

On race days when there were many extra trams, the permanent way gang went 'flagging'. They had green and red flags and were spaced out on the single line sections between the City and Weston so that there was no danger of cars meeting on single line sections and wasting time reversing.

The overhead was supported mostly on brackets varying from 6 ft to 28 ft in length on side poles painted green at first, but aluminium later; but in the city centre and some other parts, span wires with supporting rosettes were stretched from the front of houses. Round wire of hard drawn copper was used initially, O/O B & S gauge and then about 1914 figure 8 section was adopted, of ¾in. diameter. Overhead lasted 10 to 15 years on the Newton road, but only three to four years in the city centre. Guard wires were of stranded galvanised steel and earthed through poles, every third pole in the guard wire section being bonded to the rails. Ears were of the ordinary type and both mechanical and pull-off frogs were used. Later automatic switches made by Brecknell, Munro & Rogers Ltd operated by the trolley moving a drop arm. The average length of the sections was half a mile, some of the section boxes containing feeder pillars. The distribution system comprised 7¾ miles of paper-insulated and lead-covered cable supplied by British Insulated & Helsby Cables Ltd. There were 8¼ miles of overhead telephone and testing wire. The BET owned a four-wheel horse-drawn cable drum carrier.

When the Bath & West Show was at Odd Down in 1927, insulators were fixed and an extra copper wire put on to give additional feed. About 1925 automatic reversers (a triangular formation of wires to reverse the direction of the trolley and lead it from one wire to another) were installed at Bathford, Oldfield Park, Combe Down, Twerton and Newton (but not at Weston), to obviate the difficulty of turning the trolley, as it was not unknown for it to be placed on the wrong wire in the dark. At first, during busy periods, a boy was stationed at Nile Street to signal cars round the single track double bend, but then Brecknell, Munro & Rogers colour light signals were installed on single line curves at Nile Street, Kingsmead Square, Terrace Walk and

The switchboard in the power station, photographed in 1903. It was made by British Westinghouse Electric & Manufacturing Co. Ltd.   *Author's Collection*

Car 14 standing outside the tramway company's office in Northgate Street on 10th September, 1937. The office, hidden by the tram, was at No. 10 between Horton Brothers' and Roch and Cooling's shops. A cash bag has been placed on the handbrake to prevent the motorman's hand becoming dirty.   *H.B. Priestley*

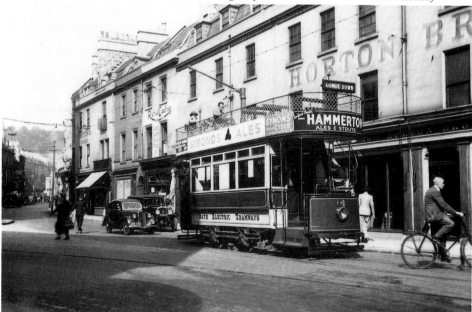

Walcot Street (St Michael's Church to the depot). It is said that Bath was used for a trial of Brecknell's switch. Until 1915, red–green lights at Bailbrook Lane and George & Dragon, Batheaston, were manually operated by a boy stationed at Bailbrook Lane. When automatic traffic lights were installed at the six road junction at the Old Bridge, other road vehicles operated them by pads set in the road. A Brecknell switch was used to work a contact on the overhead so that trams could operate the lights; trams were allowed 19 seconds to get through and it took the overhead engineers quite a long time to adjust it to this period.

Overhead engineers used a Rawlinson tower wagon pulled by a horse, or sometimes by a Bath Tramways lorry. About 1929 a spare AEC lorry was converted to a tower wagon; it drew a bogie behind it for transporting poles. Wire renewing was done on Saturday nights, as trams did not start until 10 am Sunday morning — this gave the men enough time to erect ½ mile of wire between one section box and the next. Using its expertise and equipment the tramway put in new street lights for the Corporation in 1937–8 and also dealt with any of the Corporation's sewer ventilating poles.

The finials on the standards weighed 30–40 lb., and in the 1920s one by the Abbey fell. Consequently as a precaution, all the finials were sawn off and were replaced by wood chocks. The lower ornaments were bumped off with a sledgehammer and also the scroll work. This was done during 1924–6. Some poles were found to be full of water, and when a hole was drilled to let it out, a jet sometimes shot halfway across the road.

The Power Station

The power station site was called the Beehive Yard. Three Babcock & Wilcox boilers were coupled to three Yates & Thom compound engines driving three 200 kW. Westinghouse DC generators. A Westinghouse compound engine drove a 75 kW.DC plant. The three large sets were for feeding the tramway system and the small one was an auxiliary for the traction system and for lighting the depot, and later the bus garage and the manager's house at Kensington. There were also two 15 kW Westinghouse boosters. The power station was alongside the depot, but at a much lower level.

In the early days, coal was a mixture of Ashton Vale (Bristol) and Welsh small, but later coal came from either Old Mills, or New Rock colliery near Radstock. Old Mills had bigger lumps and did not burn so well, and stokers, mostly ex-Royal Navy men, preferred New Rock as it was quicker burning. In the morning there was a stoker for each boiler and in the busier afternoon shift a stoker and a trimmer. During the early shift (6 am–2 pm) approximately 3 tons of coal were used; the afternoon shift (2 pm–10 pm) used about 5 tons whilst the night shift (10 pm–6 am) only needed 1 ton. In 1922 equipment was installed so that oil could be burnt in the event of a coal shortage caused by the miners' strike, and for a few weeks the boilers were oil fired.

The engine room was kept spotlessly clean, the machines being rubbed over every day, the flywheels cleaned once a month and the switchboard about once every three months — it could only be done on a Sunday before

10 am. Every August Bank Holiday the river was let down and this meant that the economiser could not be used as the inlet did not reach the water and consequently mains water was used. When the river was low they 'ran on atmosphere' and as a consequence of the steam escaping to the air, working was much noisier and coal consumption rose.

To start an engine, the big end was put at the top of dead centre, the main steam valve was opened and the flywheel given a kick with a steel bar fitted into the block holes on the flywheel rim.

The steel chimney of the power station was 120 ft high, a very prominent landmark. During a severe gale on 11th January, 1920 the topmost 12 ft, after swaying, was blown off and fell with a terrific crash onto the roof of the boiler house.

Dimensions of Boiler and Engine

Heating surface: 3140 sq. ft
Normal evaporation: 11,000 lb./hr
Maximum evaporation: 13,000 lb./hr
Steam pressure: 160 lb.sq.in. (some accounts say 150)
Grate Area: 59½ sq.ft
Tubes — (14 sections of 10) — 18 ft by 4 in.
Superheater: 339 sq.ft
2 condensers each 1,410 sq.ft
Economiser — Clay Cross 240 9 ft tubes.
Westinghouse DC generators, 8 pole, developing pressure of 500–550 volts.
Yates & Thom engines:
    320 hp horizontal tandem engines, single crank, compound, cyls 15 in. × 30 in. and 30 in. × 30 in. diameter
    16 ft flywheel, weight 18 tons
Westinghouse high speed engine:
    11 in. × 11 in. and 19 in. × 11 in. cyls 4 pole 75 kW.DC 550 volts.

The Depot

The eight-road car shed measured 130 ft long by 82 ft wide, with offices over the street end. All roads had pits 30 ft in length; 5 ft deep for half this distance where a wall separated the remaining 15 ft which was 15 ft in depth. Cleaners were allowed to wash cars over the shallow pits, but not over the deep pits where motors were stored underneath. At the lower end of No. 2 road the armatures were changed. The cars were well maintained and kept as good as new. When a car had wheels which had been re-tyred, it was put on the Twerton road for a week to get the flanges smooth, and then ran to Combe Down. As the tyres wore, they were taken out and turned. Finally they were used on Oldfield Park cars, which were single-deckers, and to make up for the smaller wheel diameter, these cars had bigger pinions and the first notch of the magnetic brake was inoperative. The wheel diameter when new was 32½ in., and tyres were allowed to wear down to 29¾ in. before being replaced. Re-wheeling was done on No. 7 road as this was the only one with removable rails. Tyres lasted about five years. Armatures were taken out and rewired in the fitting shop below the car shed. To haul heavy components up from the shop below, a car was attached to a rope round a pulley block and when the car was moved, the load was raised.

Men employed in the fitting shop were: a blacksmith and mate; turner (for bearings) and mate; electrician and mate; wheel turner; two fitters and two mates. The carpenters did their repairs at the far end of No. 3 road. Bodies were overhauled approximately every four years. There were about seven car cleaners. In the early days, ex-horse bus drivers were taken on as cleaners. Each man cleaned four cars and if they were particularly clean, he was paid an extra 5s. a week. His normal pay was 18s. a week, sometimes day and sometimes night work. The two controller cleaners did odd numbered cars one night and even numbers the next. Before the War, handrails and controller tops were kept polished by a Brasso boy every night. During the War the handrails were painted to save labour. Two men checked the brakes daily. The cast iron brake shoes came from the tramway's own foundry. Two men and one mate were on trolley head maintenance. Three cars were usually out of commission: one being painted; one re-wheeled and the third with motor trouble. When working on a car in the depot a board was hung on the dash 'This car must not be moved' in red letters on a white ground. Another board with white letters on a black ground read 'This car can be moved but is not available for service'. There was also in the workshops a strange vehicle resembling a wheelbarrow, with a magnetic track brake which was used for picking up nuts and bolts and scrap metal from the floor.

BATH ELECTRIC TRAMWAYS, LIMITED.

Balfour House. 119-125, Finsbury Pavement.

London: 24th June 190 8.
E.C.

TELEGRAPHIC ADDRESS,
TRAMMELETS.LONDON."

25 JUN 1908

W. E. Hardy, Esq.,
Power Station,
Walcot Street,
BATH.

Dear Sir,

Bath Electric Tramways Limited letterhead.

Car 14 leaving Weston terminus for the GWR station on 27th July, 1938. Then a village, Weston has now become a suburb of Bath. *H.B. Priestley*

At St James' Church in Southgate Street, 1925: No. 25 is working GWR station–Weston; No. 9 is on the Guildhall–Twerton duty; and an unidentified car proceeds from the Lower Borough Walls to the GWR station. *Author's Collection*

Chapter Six
Operation

The car controls were in the standard positions: handbrake, right; starting handle (forward, neutral, reverse) centre; and the controller handle on the left. As with most controllers, one could only travel any distance on the fifth or eighth notch. The motorman fed up slowly from notch to notch, or the switch blew with a loud noise. If it did, the driver (or conductor if it was his end), knocked it in. The motorman threw off power when he arrived at the insulated piece at a section box.

The magnetic brake was used on hills as the handbrake was unable to stop a loaded car on a gradient. If the rail was greasy, sand was dropped before braking, or the wheels would lock and cause a 'flat'. Nearing a terminus, the motorman would often gong for the conductor to apply the handbrake, though it was really the driver's job to stop the car, and only when it was stopped should the conductor's brake have been applied. The sand hoppers were operated by a pedal and only those at the leading end dropped sand. On hot days, tar ran on the rails particularly on hills, and plenty of sand was needed. An emergency box of sand was kept under the stairs.

When a motorman booked on, he was given the key of the tool box under the stairs and took out his driving handle, controller handles, two sand pedals, duster and handbrush. Handles and pedals were fitted and dust which had collected since the cleaners finished, brushed out. He switched off the current and opened the controller box, then tested forward and reverse; tested the magnetic brake; inspected the sand boxes and checked that there were spare bags under the seats, then turned the trolley and checked that the canvas seat covers were folded. The conductor meanwhile had collected and checked his tickets and waybills. Leaving or entering the depot, the conductor had to walk behind holding the rope to make sure the trolley stayed on — if it had brought down all the wires, the trams would have been boxed in.

Drivers had a brownish-red running card covered with shellac to waterproof it, and this was hung by the stairs. This card instructed him where to pass other cars. If when a loop was reached another car was not in sight, a motorman went on and 'rushed him a loop'. If a motorman became late he had to work hard to get time back as if he was 'rushed a loop' he had to wait for the other car and then would be caught in a vicious circle. The running card also instructed motormen of certain cars to stop at the timekeeper's office at the depot to pick up a board which read: 'This car connects with bus to . . . ' These boards were cream with blue lettering. The cars had a holder for route plates to hang below the canopy; the first car on a route bore a '1'; the next '2' and so on. Route plates were discontinued about 1925.

A conductor wishing to become a driver had to obtain a driving permit and learn in his spare time. After tuition, usually several hundred hours, the chief inspector tested him. Coming down from Devonshire Buildings an emergency stop was made and if the practical test, *viva voce*, written and medical examination were satisfactory, he became a spare driver. In the early days spare drivers had to arrive at 4.15 am and wait until the last duty left at 3.45 pm and if no one was away, then they had no turn and there was

Car 28 and Milnes-Daimler bus No. FB 05 exchanging passengers at Harris' Farm, Bathford, *c*.1908. The wooden notice on the pole bears the legend 'Alight here for motor omnibuses', with an enamel sign 'All Cars Stop Here' above it. There is a waiting room behind and just to the left of the signpost.   *M.J. Tozer Collection*

Car 6 in Kingsmead Street; it has a hospital board at the foot of the centre window (1939).   *S. Miles Davey*

no pay. Spare men sometimes begged regular men to stay away so that they could earn money. Later a 48 hour week was guaranteed to spare drivers upgraded from the company's conductors and a 32 hour week for new drivers. If spare men worked on the last shift, finishing at 12.5 am they would sometimes sleep in the car so that they would be on the spot at 4.15 am. Such was the rate of sacking in the early days, that a driver was only on the spare list for a few weeks before he became a regular driver.

A passed driver went to the Oldfield Park or Twerton routes and then when a vacancy occurred, he went to another road: once he was assigned to his final road, he kept to it. Weston, Newbridge Road and Newton formed one section and Combe Down and Bathford another. Combe Down was the most popular road as time passed quickly since it took almost two hours to do a round trip, but it had 60 duties, which meant that the men's mealtimes were the same only once in 60 weeks. One awkward turn involved four hours on the Oldfield Park road, followed by four hours to Twerton, and if the motorman was not thinking, it was all too easy to try to take a double-decker Twerton car under the Green Tree arch. On Oldfield Park, crews had to work eight hours without a break, and they arranged with other motormen that on certain trips they would be early so that they could snatch a few minutes to drink their tea. There were several shops and houses on the tram routes which provided crews with a bottle of tea.

The Lower Bristol Road from the Old Bridge to the Green Tree, and even as far as the bottom of Brougham Hayes, was flooded every few years and when it was too deep for trams to pass through, a shuttle service was run to either end of the flood. The Oldfield Park car and the Twerton car were stabled at the top and bottom of Brougham Hayes in such times and a watchman went up and down keeping an eye on both cars. Sometimes during floods, a bus service was substituted using an alternative route.

If a motorman found himself on a 'dead' rail where dirt prevented a circuit being made, he would scrape the rail clean ahead of his car, put one end of his point bar on the rail, drop the other end on the fender to complete the circuit and the car went forward. As it did so, his conductor had to give a smart tug to a piece of string tied to the bar, or it would have gone straight through the dash. Point bars were used in a similar way for re-railing a car which had gone off the end of the line at a terminus.

Drivers were given a bonus of 26s. every half year for looking after the cars — if a scratch appeared on a tram and the motorman was unable to report who was responsible, he was fined 2s. 6d. Children scratched the panels with matches and sticks. A fine was incurred for damaging the boom's insulation and a motorman would try and smooth the insulation down with his controller handle, or if he could not, he found that slipping one of the depot men some money for a pint of beer, was cheaper and easier than putting in a report and paying a fine. A 2s. 6d. fine was imposed for pulling out a trolley head and 1s. fine for slight damage to the boom.

If an employee was on the suspension list he had to go before the super-intendent. It was unfortunate if he was on an early turn, as this caused him to miss a day's work whether he was guilty or not. One conductor was on the suspension list for a miss-fare when carrying 73 passengers. Suspensions

Car 7 at the Weston terminus *c.*1912, perhaps about to carry a Sunday School outing; its side destination board read 'Via Midland Rly'. The linen has 'GW Rly Station' instead of the more usual 'GWR Station'. Seat covers can be seen by the netting above the advertisements.
Author's Collection

No. 11 to Weston outside the GWR station. There are two posters advertising the 1935 edition of *Holiday Haunts* below the 'Way Out' sign. The footbridge to the rear of the tram connected the up platform directly with the Royal Hotel.
B.Y. Williams

were given for having a button undone, or not turning the destination linen. The company could afford to be strict, as when there was a vacancy for a conductor, 50 men were sent up from the Labour Exchange.

The cars used to carry as many people as possible and one conductor remembers that the last car of the evening to Bathford once held 121 passengers — they were standing inside, on the back stairs, upstairs, down the front stairs and on the front platform. On the rear platform the gate had to be closed to keep them on. Ninety passengers have been carried on a single-decker.

Conductors were required to use the bell to ring off at a fare stage, to face the rear keeping a sharp look out for intending passengers, but at intermediate stops could blow a whistle — some conductors were provided with pea whistles and some with the tubular type — but unofficially conductors often stamped on the floor, or banged the advertisement panels. At a terminus the conductor would shout, 'Front way out, please' and in the early days at the Guildhall passengers had to alight at the motorman's end, while passengers boarded at the other end.

A general speed limit of 8 mph was imposed over the whole system, though 14 mph was permitted on the Turnpike–Newton section; 12 mph between Bannerdown Road and Bathford, and Newbridge Hill to Weston; 10 mph was permitted along certain flat stretches and a restriction of 4 mph imposed on sharp curves and all facing points. Compulsory Board of Trade stops were situated at dangerous crossroads and at the head of steep gradients.

Snow occasionally disrupted services, for example on 17th January, 1926 the first car for Combe Down left the Guildhall at 12.30 pm, and with Hardy and his men clearing away snow and ice, reached the terminus, 3¾ miles away at 4.00.

Traffic

The following were the results of the first two years of working:

	1904	1905	+ or −
Units generated	1,227,200	1,411,900	+184,700
Cost per unit	·635d.	·511d.	−·124d.
Single track miles	16	19	+3
Car mileage	900,200	967,600	+67,400
Passengers carried	6,648,100	6,746,300	+98,200
Times population carried	85·68	87	+1·32
Cost per car mile	5·268d.	4·791d.	−·477d.
Receipts per car mile	8·831d.	8·654d.	−·177d.
per cent costs to receipts	59·65%	55·36%	−4·29%
Average miles per car per day	89	99	+10
Advertisement receipts	£616	£852	+£236
Parcels	£346	£660	+£314

In 1906 the first year of full opening, 1,130,960 car miles were run and 7,082,072 passengers carried, the average number of passengers per car being 15·21. In 1905 and 1906 a dividend of 5 per cent was declared. From

No. 23 stands at the GWR station on 18th April, 1938. Although the trolley pole has been turned, the destination linen has yet to receive attention. The footbridge between the station and the Royal Hotel, depicted on *page 72*, has now been removed.

W.A. Camwell

Despite the destination linen, No. 55 is heading across the Old Bridge towards the Guildhall *c.*1905. Notice the points boy to the left of the car, and the police and fire station under the railway viaduct. The picture shows the lovely ornamental stonework which the GWR installed along this side of its viaduct, facing the City, for quite a long distance, and most of which still survives today, although the opposite side, not visible from the City, never did have such treatment.

Bath Reference Library

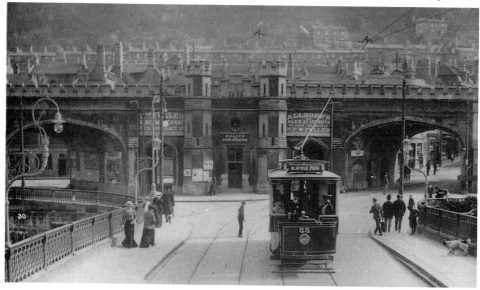

Car 10 at The Globe Inn, Newton St Loe, on 18th April, 1938. The automatic trolley reverser can be seen to the right. A tram terminus in such a rural position was unusual, but it was within a short walking distance of the villages of Corston and Newton. *W.A. Camwell*

Oldfield Park, Twerton and Guildhall cars on the Old Bridge, *c*.1939. Southgate Street is visible on the right. *Gilbert Mortimer*

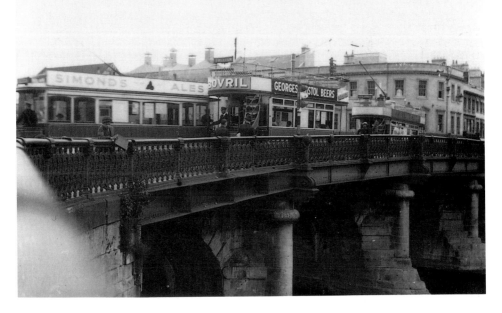

then on, no dividend was paid until the initial debentures were paid off. In 1912 the Bath & West Agricultural Show at Odd Down attracted many visitors and in five days, 160,560 passengers were carried on the trams and 22,980 on the buses. This helped the company in 1913 to pay off £5,000 debentures and they were able to place £10,000 in the renewals and contingency account then standing at £18,000 for the anticipated track re-laying in seven years time, though in 1920 it cost £12,000 to take up and relay a mile of track. The weather affected tramway receipts — at Easter 1918 between Friday and Monday 115,000 passengers were carried, but with better weather at Easter 1919, 150,000 passengers were carried over the same period. A dividend of 2½ per cent was declared in 1925 — the first since 1906. This dividend was not paid out of tramway working but out of the dividend of the interests of the company, mainly the £24,840 invested in the Bath Tramway Motor Co. Ltd. 2½ per cent was paid again in 1926 and the following year rose to 3½ per cent which continued despite the trade depression, unemployment and the opening of Oldfield Park and Bathford halts in 1929 introducing rail competition. The dividend was increased to 4 per cent in 1935.

Rules and Regulations

Conductors were required to keep their cars clean, swept and dusted and the windows and brasswork clean and bright. 'In wet weather especially, the platforms and steps must be frequently swept.' They were required to turn the cushions on workmen's cars. Five beats on the motorman's gong was the signal for the conductor to apply immediately the rear brakes. The company went all out to get traffic and required that when 'passing churches, theatres, or places of public resort, Conductors should bring the car to a full stop, if necessary'. 'Their entire time and attention is required in receiving passengers; providing seats; assisting elderly persons, ladies and children, in getting in and out; politely attending to those who may wish to enter or leave a car.' When not collecting fares, they were expected to face the rear.

'Each day before leaving the Depot all Motormen must sign for one hauling chain, one point bar, and a box containing the following materials: Spanner, Screwdriver, Oil-can, Pliers, Duster, Floorbrush, two Sand-pedals, set of Controller handles, Lighting Fuse, Wire, Lamp, and piece of Insulated Cable.' Before leaving the depot the motorman was required to see that the grease caps were filled; the controllers, motors and brushes were in order, and the sandboxes filled.

In fog, drivers had to sound their gongs: cars going from the power house sounded two gongs and those going towards it, one gong.

Uniform

Motormen and conductors wore navy blue serge uniform with red piping and brass buttons. Necks were open at first, then the uniform was required to

Car 30 at The Globe Inn, Newton St Loe, tram terminus c.1905. The authorised but unbuilt route to Saltford would have turned to the right by the big tree and continued for another 1⅝ miles.

M.J. Tozer Collection

129

Bath Electric Tramways, Ltd.

LEARNERS' PERMIT.

to _Jan 3rd_ 191 5

This entitles _____ 8 miles

to learn ~~Conducting~~ Driving with... _____ Greenof

E Seckenfs

Traffic Superintendent.

Every facility must be given to the bearer of this Permit for learning; but unless it is marked "over all routes," none but the Conductor Motorman stated above is allowed to give instruction.

To the Traffic Superintendent.

I hereby certify that the above man is now qualified to act as Motorman Conductor

_____ Inspector.

Date _____ 191

A tram driving Learner's Permit issued to Hubert Miles.

be buttoned up to the neck with two hooks and had to be secured even in hot weather. The dye caused pimples round the neck so many wore a white scarf. Jackets had two breast pockets. About 1935 double-breasted uniforms were issued and collars and black ties sold at cost price (ties cost 9d.); if a coloured tie was worn, a man was sent home. A new uniform was issued every three years. Some wore breeches and leggings (they had to buy their own leggings) and others trousers. Drivers and conductors were issued with a double-breasted overcoat. Until the 1930s 'B.E.T.C.' was stitched on their coats, but then metal badges were introduced.

Motormen were exposed and needed warm, dry clothing. Paper, either brown, or newspaper, was worn by some drivers under their coats as insulation. They used to be given the tip when the police were selling their capes and a driver bought one for 2s. 6d. — saying they were 'the best pal they had'. The cape was so thick that one would stand up by itself — the motormen usually had two, so that one could be left at home to dry. The county police capes were better quality than the city ones, but were shorter in length. The BET supplied a black, heavy oilskin cape, and with a police cape over this, the drivers never got wet. The oilskins cracked and let water in at the arms, so to prevent this, the motormen treated them with lampblack and linseed oil. Inspector Pitt designed a tarpaulin apron to go from the dash to the driver's neck, but this was not successful as it caused the driver's cap to blow off and caused a draught at his back. In the early days, the motormen and conductors wore plain caps, while inspectors had 'Inspector' embroidered on in yellow cursive lettering. From May to September caps had a white cloth cover and inspectors wore straw caps. In later days, the company issued drivers with sou'westers for wet weather.

While conductors wore black boots, most motormen preferred black clogs as these kept their feet warmer than boots. One driver who favoured boots, always took a new pair to a repairer to have a 'clump' — a thick piece of leather — nailed on the sole to keep his feet warmer. Black was essential; one man came in wearing brown as his others were being repaired, and he was sent home.

Woollen mittens were worn for warmth with leather strapped over the palms to stop the controller and brake handles wearing them out. Other drivers preferred to wear mittens of five or six pieces of cloth sewn together and these kept their hands warm even when wet. In hot weather, a copper, or silver money bag slipped over the brake handle prevented the hands from becoming black. One driver preferred a chamois leather bag instead and others wore a leather hand strap with two buckles to save their palms getting sore.

Conductresses wore a navy blue costume consisting of a three-quarter length coat, skirt, peaked cap and brown gaiters. Difficulties were experienced in getting the uniform supplied and it was not issued until 1st December, 1915.

Nos. 4, 32, 16, 14, 1, 50 and 22 rest in the depot, in 1939. *S. Miles Davey*

Nos. 6 and 9 in the depot, with the water car on the extreme right, 10th September, 1937. *H.B. Priestley*

A line-up of cars in Walcot Street depot: Nos. 16, 8, 52 and 32 on 10th September, 1937. The pits can be seen in the foreground.

J. P. Priestley

Wages

In the early days, conductors were paid 4¼d. an hour and after eighteen months this was increased to 4½d. making £1 2s. 6d. for a 60 hour week; 2d. a week was docked for recreation (papers etc.). The recreation room was above the ticket office in Southgate Street. If a man was two minutes late, he lost his pay as a spare man took his place. When a motorman was passed out he earned 5½d. an hour; after six months' satisfactory driving, if he wrote asking for it, he was paid 6d. an hour — £1 10s. 0d. for a 60 hour week.

In 1919 a conductor was paid £2 8s. 0d. and a motorman £2 15s. 0d. for a 60 hour week, though in March that year, the hours were reduced to 48 for the same remuneration. In 1932 motormen were paid 1s. 1d. an hour, £2 12s. 0d. for a 48 hour week, and conductors 1s. 0½d. (£2 10s. 0d.), while bus drivers were paid 1s. 2d. an hour.

Conductresses were paid from £1 9s. 0d. to £1 11s. 6d. a week, but from 9th July, 1918 this was raised by 5s.

Timetables

After conductors had collected fares, they were expected to call out 'Timetables, ½d. each'. The price was raised to 1d. in 1917. The various routes were colour-coded in the timetable, but from May 1926, this useful practice ceased; however, the new style timetable gave itineraries of interesting walks from termini at Combe Down, Bathford and Newton.

At the beginning of operation, some Bathford and Lambridge cars went up and down Broad Street, others using Walcot Street both ways, but from an early date they all ran up Broad Street (northbound) and down Walcot Street (southbound), and this method continued until 1939.

In January 1907, the first car left the Guildhall for Combe Down at 4.47 am and took a journey time of 30 minutes, while the first car to Bathford left the Guildhall at 5.0 am and took 24 minutes, most cars taking 54 minutes Bathford–Combe Down, a distance of 7 miles. From 6.30 am several cars ran Lambridge–Combe Down and from 8.22 am a service ran every 16 minutes Lambridge–Devonshire Arms. Together with the 16 minute interval service Bathford–Combe Down, an 8 minute service was provided Lambridge–Devonshire Arms, with a 7 minute frequency in the late afternoon and early evening. The last through car left Bathford at 10.37 pm and the last car from Bathford arrived at the Guildhall at 11.54, or 12.4 am with the extra Saturday working. From Combe Down cars arrived at the Guildhall at 12.5 am or 12.15 on Saturdays. The Sunday service was about every 15 minutes from 11 am until about 10.30 pm.

Usual times taken for the journey were:

Bathford–Lambridge 12 mins, later 10 mins up and 11 mins down.
Lambridge–Guildhall 12 mins, later 10 mins up and 11 mins down.
Guildhall–Devonshire Arms 15 mins up and 14 mins down (later 12 each way).
Devonshire Arms–Combe Down 15 mins up and 16 mins down, (later 14 mins up, and 15 mins down).
('Up' was from Bathford to Combe Down, and 'down' the reverse direction.)

Bath Electric Tramways.

Head Office, 10 Northgate Street.   Tel. 1214.

Guildhall to Bathford.

6.0, 6.28, 7.0 (7.19 1am.), 7.29, (7.41, Lam.), 7.60, 8.18, every 20 m. till 11.36am, every 14 m. till 10.6pm., then 10.22 (Batheaston only), 10.30, 10.45 (last car).

Saturday—Same as above till 10.40 am, then 10.36 am, every 15 m. till 10.30 pm, 10.45 (last car).

Sun.—10.0 (10.20 Lambridge only), 10.39, 10.56, 11.15, every 20 m. till 1.55, then 2.6, every 10 m. till 6.0, every 15 m. till 6.0, every 14 m. till 10.6pm.

Devonsh. Bdgs. to Lambridge.

6.38, 7.5, 7.30, 8.1, 8.21, 8.8b, every 10 m. till 11 55, then every 7 m. till 10.30pm.

Guildhall to Coombe Down.

5.50, 6.20, 6.47, 7.0, 7.16, 7.46, 8.10, every 20 m. till 11.30, then every 14 m. till 10 0 pm, then 10.16, 10.30, 10.46 pm. Also alternate cars to Glasshouse between 2.11 and 7.47

Saturday—Same service till 10.30, then every 14 m. till 12.50pm, then every 7 m. till 10.46 pm. (last car).

Sunday— 9.60 (9.57 G'house only) 10.20, every 20 m. till 2.0 pm., every 10 m. till 6.0, every 15 m. till 6.0, every 14 m. till 9.68, then till 10.6 pm.

G.W.R. to Upper Weston.

7.16, 7.31, 7.55, 8.10, every 20 m. till 11.50, then 12.8, every 16 m. till 8.40, then 9.0, every 20 m. till 10.20, 10.37 last car.

Fridays—Same service till 1.12, then 1.27, every 14 m. till 8.41, then 9.0, every 20 m. till 10.20, 10.30 last car.

Saturdays—Same service till 9.60 a.m., then 10.8, every 16m. till 12.0, every 12m. till 10.24, 10.37, 10.46 last car.

Sundays—10.12, 10.24, every 24 m. till 1.56, 1.64, 2.7, then every 16m till 10 7 pm (last car).

Bathford to Guildhall.

6.25, 7.3 (Lam.), 7.23, 7.32 (Lam.), 7.52, 7.52 (Lam.), 8.20, every 20 m. till 11.40, then 11.58am, and every 14 m. till 10.28, 10.39 (Batheaston), 10.52, 11.7 pm.

Saturday—Same service till 10.58, every 14 m. till 10.52, 11.7.

Sunday—10.30, 10.69, every 20 m. till 2.0, then 2.20, every 10 m. till 5.8, then 5.23, every 16 m. till 6.0, every 14 m. till 10.33 p.m.

Lambridge to Devonsh. Bdgs.

6.36, 7.3, 7.34, 8.4, 8.18, 8.30, every 10 m. till 12.1, then every 7m. till 10.32pm.
Cars extended to G'house from 2.1 to 7.37pm.

Coombe Down to Guildhall.

6.20, 6.58, 7.15, 7.30, 7.46, 8.20, every 20 m. till 11.40, then 11.58 am, every 14 m. till 10.28, 10.43, 10.58 11.13pm Also alternate cars from Glasshouse between 2.33 and 8.9.

Saturday—Same service till 10.20 am, 10.38, 10.58, every 14m. till 12.36, every 7 m. till 11.13 pm.

Sunday—(10.20 G'house only) 10.26 10.48, 11.8, every 20m. till 2.8, then 2.29, every 11 m. till 5.10, then 5.18, 5.30, every 15 m. till 6.0, every 14 m. till 10.33

G.W.R. to Upper Weston.

7.35am., 7.50, 8.16, 8.40, 9.0, 9.20, 9.30, every 20 m. till 12.0, 12.10, 12.28, every 16m. till 8.28, then 8.48, 9.10, every 20m. till 10.10, 10.20, 10.40, 10.66, last car.

Fridays—Same service till 1.45, then 2.2, every 14m. till 8.50, then 9.10, every 20m. till 10.40, 10.50 last car.

Saturdays—Same service till 10.30, 10.44, every 16m. till 12.56, every 12m. till 10.32, 10.37, 10.44, 10.57, 11.6 last car.

Sundays—10.30, 10.42, 11.17am, every 24 m. till 2.0, 2.16, 2.26 and every 16 m. till 10.26pm (last car).

Bath Electric Tramways.—*continued.*

G.W.R. to Newbridge Road.

6.0, 6.7 0.743, 8.0, every 20m till 12.0, every 16m. till 8.32, 8.50, every 20m. till 10.30, 10.45 pm.

Fridays—Same service till 1.20, every 14m. till 8.50, 9.10, every 20m. till 10.30, 10.46pm (last car).

Saturday—Same service till 10.0am., every 16 m. till 11.20, then 11.30, every 12m. till 10.30, 10.45 pm (last car).

Sunday—10.0am, 10.36, 11.0, every 24 m. till 2.0, every 16 m. till 6.42 every 12 m. till 10.0pm

G.W.R. to Newton St. Loe.

6.0am, 7.0, 8.0, 8.40, 9.20, 10.0, 10.40, 11.20, 12.0, 12.48, 1.20, 2.0, 2.40, 3.12, 3.28, 4.0, 4.16, 4.32, 4.48, 5.4, 5.20, 5.36, 5.62, 6.8, 6.24, 6.40, 7.12, 7.28, 8.0, 8.60, 9.30, 10.10 (10.46 Wed. & Sat) Sundays—10am, 11.0, 11.48, 12.12, 12.36, 2.0, and every 30 m. till 1'0pm.

Guildhall to Twerton.

6.46 a.m., 6.16, 6.56, 7.16, 7.30, 7.46, then 8.7, and every 16 min. till 12.24, then 12.36, and every 10 min. till 8.16, then every 15m. till 10.30, 10.45 pm. (last car).

Saturday—Same service till 10.7, then 10.20, and every 10m. till 5.10, then 5.18, and every 8 m. till 11.0 then (last car).

Sunday—10.10, 10.30, every 20 m. till 2.10, then 2.22, every 16 m. till 7.52, then 8.6, every 10 m. till 10.6

Guildhall to Oldfield Park.

6.20 am 7, 7.18, 7.28 7.35, 7.46 then every 15 m. till 10.30, 10.45 pm (last car).

till 4.0 pm., every 8 min. till 8.0 pm.then every 10 m. till 10.30, 10.45 (last car).

Saturday—Same service till 10.16. 10m. till 11.55, then 12.2, every 6 & 7m. till 10.45pm. (last car).

Sunday—10 20, every 20 m. till 2.20, every 10 m. till 10.10

Newbridge Road to G.W.R.

6.39, 7.39.8.5.8.31, 8.50, 9.10, 9.40, every 20m. till 12.20, 12.36, every 16m. till 8.37, 8 48, 9.1, every 20m till 10.1, 10.15, 10.41, 10.50, 11.5 (not Wed.), 11.16 (Wed. only).

Fridays—Same service till 1.46, then 1.56, every 14 m. till 8'40, 8.41, every 20 m. till 10.1, 10.16 10.41, 10.50, 11.5 (not Wed.), 11.16 (Wed).

Saturday—Same service till 11.0.38, then 10 56, every 16m. till 12.12, 12.26, every 12m. till 10.50, then 11.16 (last car).

Sundays—10.36am., 11.5, 11.30, every 24 m. till 1 30, 1.62, 2.12, 2.33, every 15m. till 10. 3, then 11.6, 10.33pm.

Newton St. Loe to G.W.R.

6.30am	2.30	8.26	9.6,	9.52,	1.61,
10.12	11.62	12.30pm		1.18,	1.61,
2.39,	3.1,	3.69,	4.31,	4.47,	5.19,
5.35,	5.7,	6.7,	6.23	6.39,	6.65,
7.11,	7.43,	7.59,	8.31,	9.16,	9.65,
10.35, 11.10pm. (Wed. & Sat.)

Sundays—10.28am, 11.24, 12.12, 12.36, 1.0, 2.26, and every 30m. till 10.-10.6p m.

Twerton to Guildhall.

6.0, 6.30, 7.0, 7.16, 7.30, 7.46, 8.6, then 8.22, and every 16m. till 12.37, then 12.50, and every 10m. till 8.30, every 15m. till 10.46, 11.0pm. (last car).

Saturday—same service till 10.6, then 10.26, and every 10m. till 5.26, then 6.34, and every 8 m. till 11.0 pm. (last car).

Sunday—10.25, 10·40, every 20 m. till 2.25, then 2.37, every 15 m. till 8.20, then 8.6, every 10 m. till 10.16. 10.20 last car

Oldfield Park to Guildhall.

6.36, 7.30, 7.50, 7.40, 7.50, 8.0, and every 16m. till 12.16, then every 10 m. till 4.15, every 8 m. till 8.16, then every 10 m. till 10.45, 11.0pm., (last car).

Saturday—Same service till 10.30, then every 10m. till 12.10, then 12.18, every 6 & 7m. till 11.0 (last car).

Sunday—10.36, every 20 m. till 2.36, every 10 m. till 10.26

Service 13			am		pm		pm
Bath and Malmesbury							

		am		pm				
Grand Parade	dep	7 50		4 15	
Up. Swainswick	,,	8 2		4 30	
Cross Roads	,,	8 38		4 48	
Acton Turville	,,	8 51		5 11	
Luckington	,,	9 4		5 14	
Sherston	,,	9 15		5 28	
Easton Grey	,,	9 25		5 38	
Malmesbury	ar	9 35		5 45	

Wednesdays only

	am		pm		pm
Malmesbury	dep	9 45		5 50
Easton Grey	,,	10 9		6 14
Sherston	,,	10 16		6 21
Luckington	,,	10 29		6 34
Acton Turville	,,	10 2		6 47
Cross Roads	,,	10 53		7 30
Up. Swainswick	,,	11 15		7 55
Grand Parade	ar	11 30		

Car 7 waits outside the Guildhall *c.1910 en route* to Combe Down; there is a horse drawn tower wagon to the left of the picture. *Author's Collection*

The highest numbered car, 34, in the double-deck series, bound for Lambridge, passes a Twerton car at the Guildhall on 11th April, 1939. *J.J. Luckman*

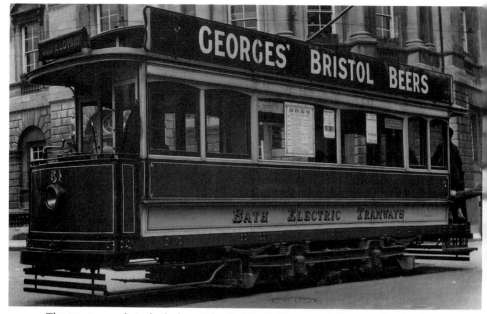

The two types of single-decker at the Guildhall: No. 51 with flatter dash. The driver sits just inside, his coat hanging on the front of the bulkhead window. Advertisements: Green Motor Coach Tours; Rugby – Bath v Portsmouth (centre window); Pump Room concert – the pianist, Kreisler (right-hand window). View c.1935.

Dr H.A. Whitcombe

No. 54 with rounded dash. Motorman Fred Styles sits just inside, his cap sporting a white summer cover. The girder below the rocker board has a different pattern of rivets than No. 51. Below are the brackets carrying the bamboo pole for use when the trolley pole required turning. The large window carried an advertisement for Green Motor Coach Tours.

W.J. Haynes

By 1917 cars for the greater part of the day ran either Bathford–Glasshouse, or Lambridge–Combe Down, while on Saturdays Lambridge–Combe Down and Bathford–Combe Down alternated, and on Sundays most cars ran Bathford–Combe Down.

For the first few weeks, the service to Newbridge Road was a shuttle service between the Weston Hotel and Bath Brewery. The Weston and Newbridge services were worked independently and although cars started from the GWR station spaced out, they eventually left the Weston Hotel or the station together and it took the BET about two years to realise they were doing a big mileage and not getting the returns they ought. In January 1907 on the Weston road the first car left the GWR station at 5.10 am and during most of the day a 14–16 minute frequency was operated with a 20–21 minute journey (later 18 mins), for the distance of 2¼ miles. Several cars terminated at the Crown Hotel. The first car to Newton left the GWR station at 5.45 am and took 29 minutes (later 24 mins out and 26 mins in), for the journey of 3¾ miles. An hourly service was run, and together with an hourly service as far as Bath Brewery, gave a 30 minute interval service GWR station–Bath Brewery. The last car to Newton left the GWR station at 10.0 pm. The last one to Bath Brewery left at 10.59 and on Saturdays this was extended to Newton.

In February 1909, Bath Brewery trams were extended to Cross Roads loop, Newbridge Road, a journey of 20 minutes from the GWR station, but after 9.15 pm the working was cut back to Rudmore Farm, a 19 minute run. Rudmore Farm ceased to be a terminus from 31st December, 1916. The time allowance at Cross Roads loop allowed a car to be sent on to Newton if an inspector ordered it and this was often done on a fine Sunday afternoon. In December 1915, late services were reduced and one car made two journeys each way Weston Hotel–Cross Roads loop, connecting with a Weston car. This continued until the end of the War. From November 1919–December 1925 a similar short working was instituted, but with only one journey each evening from Weston Hotel–Weston. In December 1925 the frequency of cars was increased during parts of the day and a special Friday timetable was introduced after 1.20 pm on the Newbridge/Weston roads, giving a 7 minute frequency GWR station–Weston Hotel instead of 8–10 minutes, but this special Friday timetable was abandoned from April 1929. On 1st January, 1927 'through' working started from Bath to Bristol using the tram to Newton, and Bristol Tramways & Carriage Co.'s bus route number 33 from Newton–Bristol. In the spring of 1928, BTCC buses started running a through service from Bristol to Bath and it was no longer necessary for passengers to change from bus to tram at Newton; however, the service of 32 cars to Newton still continued until April 1929.

In 1907 the first car Guildhall–Twerton left at 5.15 am and took 16 minutes, later 14 minutes for the journey of 2 miles. A 17 minute frequency service was run except between 1.0 and 8.27 pm when the frequency was every 12 minutes. The last car departed at 11.15 pm. On Saturdays a 9 minute service was run after 4.38 pm and every 7 minutes after 6.8. In February 1908 alterations were made to give a service of 17 more cars. All ran to the terminus until 7.35 am, but subsequently terminated at the

Car 15 at Twerton terminus on 18th April, 1938. Note the automatic trolley reverser – a triangular formation of wires – to the left beyond the car. On the extreme right is the wall of the GWR Twerton station which closed on 2nd April, 1917.   *W.A. Camwell*

Motorman Len Hancock on car 34 to Devonshire Buildings, uses a point bar at the Old Bridge. Skilful drivers could change points without stopping; 11th April, 1939.

J.J. Luckman

Railway Hotel, Twerton until 10.55 pm. The following month the Railway Hotel stop was re-named Twerton Railway Station in the timetables. In January 1918 the terminus was completely cut back to the station.

In 1907 the first Guildhall–Oldfield Park car left at 5.15 am and took 15 minutes, later 14 minutes, for its journey of 1½ miles. For most of the morning an 11 minute frequency was run until 2.20 pm and then every 8 minutes until 8.30. The last car left the Guildhall at 11.15 pm. On Saturdays there was an 8 minute frequency from 12.28 and after 4.52 pm a 7 minute frequency until the last car departed at 11.15. On Sundays cars on all routes left the city about 10 am and allowed people to reach the city churches by 11 am. On Sundays three single-deck cars worked the Oldfield Park and Twerton roads together.

So that residents in hotels would not be disturbed, before 7.45 am and after 11 pm (midnight on Saturdays), cars were not allowed to use Manvers Street and Pierrepont Street and returned up Southgate Street. On reaching the single line Cheap/Stall Street corner, the driver sent the conductor ahead to see that the road was clear.

On race days special cars ran to Weston terminus and as many as 14 would be lined up awaiting home-going race people. The racecourse itself, however, was another 1½ miles walk beyond Weston tram terminus, up the very steep hillside where a rack railway had earlier been planned. Specials were also run to football matches and horse shows at Lambridge. When the Royal United Hospital was moved to Combe Park in the 1930s, each visiting day a special was run to carry visitors, and a spare tram was ready at the GWR station in case of an overload. Special cars could be hired, and choir and Sunday School outings availed themselves of this facility, though in the later 'twenties and thirties, special cars were rare.

A new timetable introduced on 1st December, 1935 was not very different from the previous one, and continued without substantial change until the end in 1939. The main trunk route worked mostly in two overlapping sections, with very few journeys right through end-to-end. On Mondays to Fridays there were three early morning journeys departing from Combe Down at 6.20, 7.15 and 7.46 am running through to Bathford, otherwise departures from Combe Down went only as far as Lambridge, departing from Combe Down at 6.50, 8.00, then every 20 mins until 11 am, then to Lambridge every 15 mins until 9.30 pm, the 9.45 and 10.00 running through to Bathford. The 10.15, 10.30, 10.45, 11.00, and 11.15 pm ran only to the Guildhall then proceeding to the depot. Journey times from Combe Down were 8–9 mins to the Glasshouse Cafe, 15–16 mins to Devonshire Buildings, 27–30 mins to the Guildhall, 38–41 mins to Lambridge, and 52–58 mins to Bathford. To give double the frequency between Glasshouse and Lambridge, other cars departed from Glasshouse at 8.20 am and every 20 mins until 11 am, then every 15 mins until 8.17 pm, all going through to Bathford, after which cars departed from Devonshire Buildings at 8.39 pm and every 15 mins until 9.39 through to Bathford. The 9.54 pm ran only to Batheaston and the 10.09 and 10.24 only to Lambridge, the 10.38 through to Bathford, and 10.51 pm to Guildhall then proceeding to the depot.

In the opposite direction the first three morning departures from Bathford at 6.25, 6.52, and 7.23 am all worked right through to Combe Down; there

Newbridge Road, Weston.

The scene is the Weston Hotel *c*.1910 with car 14 on its way to Weston. Hoops are a popular toy; a decorator's or builder's hand cart is parked at the foot of one of the poles supporting the overhead. This picture shows the junction, to Upper Weston right, to Lower Weston and the Globe Inn left. *Author's Collection*

Car 12 at the Weston terminus photographed on 18th April, 1938. The author has taught in the school behind the tram, and plays the organ and preaches in All Saints' Church on the hill. The 'convenience' to the right of the school entrance was built for the use of tram crews, which was why it only accommodated males. *W.A. Camwell*

were six shorter journeys starting at Batheaston or Lambridge, one departure from Bathford at 7.52 to Glasshouse, and then the regular pattern started with departures from Bathford to the Glasshouse Cafe at 8.20 am and every 20 mins until 11 am, and then subsequently every 15 mins.

The twelve 15-minute departures from Bathford from 3.45 pm to 6.30 pm inclusive ran only as far as Devonshire Buildings, returning to Lambridge before going forward again to Glasshouse. This gave a regular 5-minute combined frequency between Lambridge and Devonshire Buildings during the afternoon peak period, but caused the Glasshouse cars to be every 5/10/5/10 mins during the peak instead of a regular 7½ for most of the day. After the peak the 15-minute frequency from Bathford until 7.30 pm went through to Glasshouse again, then every 15 mins from Bathford until 10.15 pm to Devonshire Buildings only, then at 10.38, 10.53, and 11.13 pm to the Guildhall for depot. Fitting in mid-way between all the Bathford journeys were the trips to Combe Down departing from Lambridge at 8.40 am and every 20 mins until 11.04 am, then every 15 mins until 10.19 pm, and 10.38 pm. However the full service at peak times needed a total of 16 cars. They all worked very hard, with terminal layovers mostly only one or two minutes, necessitated by the very long stretch of single track at the outer ends of all six Bath tram routes.

The Saturday service was the same as weekdays from the start until 12 noon, but from then onwards the cars from Combe Down to Lambridge and back ran every 14 mins instead of every 15, also the Glasshouse to Bathford cars worked every 14 mins instead of 15 and in addition they all started from Come Down. Hence the service to and from Combe Down was every 7 mins from noon until the 11.18 pm departure from Combe Down, a service more than twice as frequent as a Monday to Friday. The last departure from Bathford was 11.12 pm, to Guildhall only. The complicated short-working arrangement on the central part of the route between 4 pm and 7 pm on Mon–Fri did not apply on Saturdays.

On Sunday mornings the first car out of the depot left the Guildhall at 9.40 am and departed from Combe Down at 10.10 am while the first from Bathford was at 10.30. All cars then ran right through from Combe Down to Bathford and back every 20 mins until approx. 2 pm, and then every 10 mins until approx. 5 pm. From then onwards the overlapping procedure was adopted, with cars every 14 mins from Combe Down to Lambridge and back, also every 14 mins from Glasshouse to Bathford and back, giving a 7 minute frequency between Glasshouse and Lambridge. The last inward car departed from Combe Down at 10.43 pm (to Guildhall only), and the last from Bathford was at 10.36 pm, to Guildhall only.

The Weston and Newton St Loe services were interworked. Both started from the GWR station, and from 9 am onwards there was a regular service every 7½ mins to the Weston Hotel (time 12 mins), from where alternate cars branched every 15 mins to Weston (time 17 mins) or every 15 mins to Newbridge Cross Roads Loop (time also 17 mins). From this loop alternate cars then continued every 30 mins to Newton St Loe (time 24 mins). This regular pattern continued until 9 pm; with no extras for the peak hour. Before 9 am and after 9 pm services were slightly less frequent, but the first

A Newton to GWR station car crossing the New Bridge on 9th January, 1938.

Gilbert Mortimer

Scene at the Old Bridge, 10th September, 1937: car 50 bound for the Guildhall passes car 51 to Oldfield Park. Beyond, a double-deck car from either Newton or Weston to the GWR station is turning into Dorchester Street.

H.B. Priestley

morning cars arrived at Weston at 7.34 am and at Newton at 7.28 am, and the last evening cars at 11.07 pm and 11.09 pm respectively, all four returning 1 or 2 minutes later. Cars worked alternate journeys on each of the two routes, and a total of eight cars was needed.

The Saturday service from the GWR station was the same as weekdays until 12 noon, but for the rest of the day it was then on the basis of every 6, 12 & 24 mins instead of the 7½, 15 & 30 described above. Some of the Cross Roads journeys continued to Newton, giving Newton an irregular interval of sometimes 24 and sometimes 12 mins. The last car on Saturday night reached both Weston and Newton at 11.09 pm, returning from both destinations at 11.10. On Sunday five journeys were made each way at irregular intervals between 10 am and 11 am, then a regular pattern was worked until 2 pm of every 24 mins to Weston and every 24 mins to Newbridge, only some of which continued to Newton, and then from 2 pm until the last car from the Station (at 10.15 pm) the weekday 7½/15/30 mins frequencies applied, with the last inwards cars departing from Weston at 10.34 pm and from Newton at 10.26 pm.

The Oldfield Park and Twerton routes also shared a joint timetable, with the first car on weekday mornings leaving the Guildhall at 5.45 am. After 13 irregularly-spaced journeys before 8 am, the service then became every 15 mins on both routes, which offered a car every 7½ mins as far as the junction at the Green Tree. Running time on both routes was 7 mins to the junction and 14 mins to the outer terminus. From 12.30 pm onwards the intervals became every 5 & 10 mins instead of 7½ & 15. Oldfield Park remained every 10 mins right up until the last departure from the Guildhall at 10.50 pm, but Twerton was reduced after 8.15 pm to be every 15 mins instead of every 10, with the result that once every half hour two trams ran together in convoy from the Guildhall as far as the Green Tree. The last inward car departed from both termini at 11.05 pm.

Twelve extra cars ran to Oldfield Park between 4 pm and 7.45, some of these also resulting in two cars together as far as the Green Tree. The Twerton service required a maximum of three cars, normally all double-deckers, and Oldfield Park needed a maximum of five, which had to be single-deckers because of the low bridge under the GWR main line immediately beyond the Green Tree junction.

On Saturday Oldfield Park and Twerton had the same service as Monday to Friday until 10.15 am, after which Oldfield Park became every 10 mins until noon, then every 6 or 7 mins until 10.50 pm, whilst Twerton was every 10 mins from 10.20 am until 5.10 pm, then every 8 mins until 10.50 pm. On Sundays both routes were every 20 mins from 10 am until 2.30 pm, and then Oldfield Park became every 10 mins until 8 pm, and every 7½ mins from then until 10.15 pm from the Guildhall, whilst Twerton became every 15 mins from 2.22 pm until 8 pm, then every 10 mins until 10.15 pm. The increased frequency on both these two routes in the late evening on Sundays, much better than weekdays, is in striking contrast to the Sunday evening bus services in Bath today.

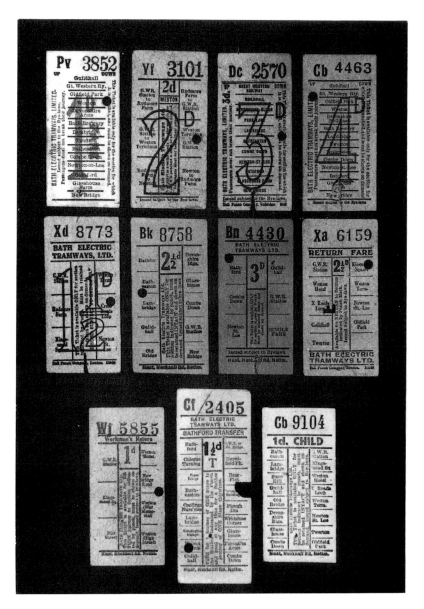

A selection of Bath Electric Tramways tickets from J. Helsdon's Collection arranged in approximate date order.

Tickets and Fares

Tram fares in 1908 on the main route were 1*d*. from Bathford to Batheaston Post Office, 1*d*. from there to Lambridge, 1*d*. from Lambridge to Old Bridge, 1*d*. from Guildhall to Devonshire Arms, 1*d*. from there to Glasshouse Farm, and 1*d*. from Bath Union to Combe Down; also 2*d*. from Bathford to Lambridge, 2*d*. from Batheaston to Old Bridge, 2*d*. from Lambridge to Devonshire Arms, 2*d*. from Guildhall to Glasshouse Farm, and 2*d*. from Devonshire Arms to Combe Down; also 3*d*. from Bathford to Old Bridge, 3*d*. from Batheaston to Devonshire Arms, 3*d*. from Lambridge to Glasshouse Farm, and 3*d*. from Guildhall to Combe Down; also 4*d*. from Bathford to Devonshire Arms, 4*d*. from Batheaston to Glasshouse Farm, 4*d*. from Lambridge to Come Down, 5*d*. from Bathford to Glasshouse Farm, 5*d*. from Batheaston to Combe Down, and 6*d*. all the way from Bathford to Combe Down. On the Newton St Loe route they were 1*d*. from GWR station to Park Lane, 1*d*. from Weston Hotel to New Bridge, 1*d*. from New Bridge to Newton, 2*d*. from Station to New Bridge, 2*d*. from Weston Hotel to Newton, and 3*d*. from Station to Newton. Fares on the three shorter routes were 1½*d*. from Station to Weston, 1*d*. from Guildhall to Twerton, and 1*d*. from Guildhall to Oldfield Park. Children between three and nine years of age travelled for half fare. The last tram from Weston or Newton would take passengers from the GWR station to the Guildhall for an extra 1*d*. on its way to the depot. In 1908 the Weston fare went up by ½*d*. as passengers were travelling 2 miles 584 yds for 1*d*. and workmen on this road nearly 5 miles for 1*d*. On race days the company were authorised to charge 2*d*. from the GWR station to Weston.

In July 1917 slight fare increases were made, and in April 1919 fares were increased by a ½*d*., but there was 1*d*. increase past the Guildhall, as either side of the Guildhall counted as two services, with through cars for convenience. Transfer fares went up 1*d*., but children's fares were not allowed to be increased. As the company found it impossible to get fresh tickets, the old tickets were used, but higher fares paid for them. i.e. 1*d*. tickets cost 1½*d*. There was another ½*d*. increase on 27th July, 1920, and workmen's fares were raised for the first time, causing the disappearance of the ½*d*. workman's single. In March 1923, 2*d*. tickets, both ordinary and transfer were reduced to 1½*d*., and 2½*d*. to 2*d*., and the maximum age for children's fare raised to twelve.

By 1931 the fares scale was 1½*d*. minimum, 2*d*., 3*d*., and 4*d*. maximum, but these were to the Guidlhall only, with no through fares advertised from the Bathford route to or from the Combe Down Route. There was also a special fare of 1*d*. between the Guildhall and Old Bridge. Children up to 14, scholars up to 18, and also dogs, were charged half the adult fares. Prepaid single tickets of 1½*d*., 2*d*., 3*d*., and 4*d*. value were sold in books of 12, but at no reduction in price. Tickets for six return journeys on 3*d*. and 4*d*. ordinary stages were however sold at reduced rates, subject to being used inside 14 days. Bicycles and perambulators were carried at ordinary adult fares.

Dorchester Street in the last week of Bath trams. No. 24 is on its way to the GWR station, the linen having already been turned for its journey to Weston; an Oldfield Park to Guildhall single-deck car is behind, while a double-deck bus, which had replaced trams on the Twerton route, brings up the rear. *S. Miles Davey*

The Guildhall terminus with car 53 ready to leave for Oldfield Park on 18th April, 1938. This car has an angular dash. The tram is unusual in having a three bar, instead of a two bar, lifeguard gate. A Twerton car stands behind No. 53. *W.A. Camwell*

In July 1932 fares for short distances were reduced in an effort to gain more traffic. On 1st January, 1936, fares fell to the pre-war level. Some tickets had 'up' or 'down' printed on them — Bathford–Combe Down was 'up' and on other routes it was 'up' to the terminus, and the conductor punched the ticket for the appropriate direction.

Workmen's returns were issued on cars leaving a terminus by 8 am, and issued to bona fide artisans, mechanics and daily labourers, costing single fare for return journey between 5–8 pm weekdays and 12 noon–2 pm Saturdays, or half price for a workman's single i.e. ½d. for a 1d. stage. Workmen's and transfer tickets were nipped with the code letter for the day (letters used were B, V, X, F, A), as well as being punched. With a transfer ticket a passenger could either return, or go on the next transfer stage on the same or another route, and so get a 3d. journey for 1½d. Inspectors' silver-plated clippers nipped an 'I'. By 1931 the scale of workmen's fares was 1d., 1½d. or 2d. single, and 2d., 2½d., 3d., or 4d. return.

From Mondays to Fridays 8d. Palace tickets were available from Combe Down, Bathford and Newton, which entitled passengers to a seat at the theatre and transport both ways, saving 4d. on separate bookings. The cost of these tickets rose to 9d. in 1916 and 10d. in 1917. From May 1907 circular tour tickets, price 2s. 6d., were issued by tram and bus from anywhere on the route Guildhall–Bathford–Bradford–Trowbridge–Frome–Norton St Philip –Glasshouse–Guildhall. The company went all out to get tourist traffic and about 1906 published a 64 page booklet on art paper, price 2d., *Visitors Guide to Bath & District by Electric Car & Motor Bus*.

In 1907 a new facility was announced:

> Brass tokens are now supplied for the convenience of Tradesmen and others who require their Employees to use the Cars. The tokens can be used in payment for a fare or fares in accordance with the user's requirements and can be purchased at their face value. The system is a very useful one for keeping a check on the petty expenditure in connection with car travelling.

Later tokens were made of vulcanite.

Weekly tickets were introduced in 1925 and issued for 3d. and 4d. stages; the former cost 2s. 3d. for six return journeys and the latter 3s., and in 1927 these tickets were not required to be used daily, but could be used over 14 days. In April 1904 scholars' tickets were sold in packets of 25 costing half adult fare for a journey; this scheme was amended to weekly scholars' tickets in 1908. Weekly tickets were not generally issued for adults, though towards the end of the system, they were issued to Bathford for workers at Monkton Farleigh ammunition store, a 1930s conversion of a former stone mine with its own internal narrow gauge railway system.

The Corporation paid for free passes for their employees who had to travel in the course of their duties, and the police travelled free. The blind had a pass on trams which, after their abolition, was only available on buses running over the ex-tram routes. Postmen had prepaid tickets — the conductor issuing an ordinary one in exchange.

Girls in the Northgate Street office made up the ticket boxes, then the depot was phoned, and a car went down to collect the boxes which were in

Bath Electric Tramways, Ltd.

PERMIT

Date *Dec 29 .06*

This entitles *Cond Withers* ① to learn

Driving with *Mrs Padfield*

P. Swinerton

MANAGER & ENGINEER.

N.B.—Drivers and Conductors on being shown this Permit must give the bearer every facility for learning

A Permit issued to allow conductor Withers to learn driving with motorman Padfield.

Ab 6644	PS

BRISTOL OMNIBUS CO. LTD.
BATH TRAMWAYS MOTOR CO. LTD.

PARCELS SERVICE

2/- PAID

THIS PORTION MUST BE AFFIXED TO THE PARCEL

ISSUED SUBJECT TO COMPANIES REGULATIONS

A parcels ticket issued post-1957 by Bristol Omnibus and Bath Tramways Motor Company, the latter running non ex-tramway routes.

BATH ELECTRIC TRAMWAYS, LTD.

NOTICE TO EMPLOYEES.

The above Engraving represents a Gold Pass, which is held by each Director of the Company. On this Pass being produced, either on Buses or Cars, Conductors will not demand any Fare.

The Pass is also available for Admission to the Car Shed, Power House and Garage, or any of the Company's Premises.

W. E. HARDY,
General Manager and Engineer.

Notice advising conductors of the validity of Directors' passes.

wooden skips, twelve boxes to a skip. They were put in routes ready for conductors to collect next morning.

In the early days tickets were printed by Bell Punch Co. Ltd and latterly by Hunt. The Bell punch was used first of all until about 1910, when the Williamson type was introduced, as it was believed the Bell punch was being 'fiddled' by conductors. When tickets were wet, a punch jammed and conductors then used punch cleaners made from hard tin. If tickets were very wet, which was unavoidable on the open top of a car, they had to be torn by hand. If a conductor was busy, to save time he might punch a ticket upside down, noting perhaps that the section for punching say 'Twerton', was on the 'E' of a Bladwell's advertisement. Smart conductors put four tickets between pairs of fingers and rang off the four in quick succession.

For most of the life of the tramway, conductors kept their tickets in bands made from garter elastic. About 1926 bus conductors who needed a greater variety of tickets started using boards with elastic nailed on as a primitive rack, and later an improved pattern of wire was made by Hubert Miles, a motorman who made them from piano wire in his spare time and charged 3d. a spring. Tram conductors gradually adopted them, but had to buy their own.

At first waybills were colour-coded for the different roads, Weston and Newton, pink; Bathford and Combe Down, white and Oldfield Park and Twerton, green, but about 1920 all waybills were white.

Parcels

The tramway parcel office was at 31, Southgate Street, to which a conductor took a parcel for other than his route. Later branch receiving offices were opened in shops in various parts of the city, and parcel messenger boys were allotted to shops for delivering them. They were paid 4s. weekly for working from 6.0 am to 6.0 pm six days a week. At 6 am they delivered papers from their parcel office to nearby houses. A horse van, later replaced by a motor van, delivered to Lansdown, Bathampton and Claverton. Early in 1907, 12, Newbridge Hill was opened as a parcel receiving office and waiting room. The company developed the parcel traffic which became a profitable sideline. Every district and village had its parcel agent and parcels were transferred from tram to bus at the Glasshouse, Harris's Farm, Bathford and Newton. When a conductor handed over a parcel to another conductor he put a yellow transfer ticket on so that its progress could be traced.

Some tram stops bore the notice 'Any Car Conductor Will Accept Parcels for Delivery in Bath & Suburbs', and conductors were supplied with a spring balance to weigh parcels. Special attention was given to the prompt delivery of milk, dairy produce, fish and meat. Parcels included small bedsteads, prams, newspapers and long lengths of timber carried up the front stairs. If a fire had broken out requiring the front stairs to be used, this could have been a source of danger. Prams and cycles behind the driver did not allow him to escape in emergency. The single-deck cars having a smaller platform could not carry so much. A conductor would be dismissed for missing delivery of a parcel, though parcel carrying had its own reward — a fishmonger would make up a packet of fish for the motorman and conductor at the end of the week for delivering his fish. The first car to Bathford picked up mail from the sorting office and delivered it to Batheaston and Bathford post offices.

About 1913 red lights were fixed outside parcel offices and if on, showed the conductor there was a parcel to collect. At the head parcel office in Southgate Street which was passed by every route, a board was dropped on a string labelled with either C, T, O, B, N, or W showing that they had a parcel for the route indicated to collect. Rates varied from 7 lb. for 1d. to 280 lb. for 1s. with double rate for carriage by bus. In October 1907 it was announced that dinners could be sent by tram to the parcel office nearest the business or school, at an average charge of ½d. a day or a minimum of 3d. a week. In later years, dinner baskets were collected direct from the cars.

In November 1909 an express messenger service and Cash on Delivery system was added to the parcel facilities. 'Visitors from the Country can have their purchases delivered to the Railway Cloak Rooms where they can be claimed upon producing the Receipt.' Express messengers were available at any time of day or night to collect anything other than letters. 'A messenger may also be employed to take luggage by Car or Cab to the Railway Station, and if required he will purchase the Railway Ticket and have the luggage labelled ready for intending passengers.'

'A Messenger may also be engaged by the hour, day or week, to deal with programmes and tickets at Concerts etc. or as a Door Attendant at Soirées and Dances, or as Door Attendant at an "At Home" and on such occasions the Messenger is provided with a special Uniform.' The page boy service ended in 1915.

Special messengers could be engaged from any of the company's depots to wait in the queues of either the early or ordinary doors of the theatre, at the rate of 6d. an hour, 'An easy and certain method of securing good seats'.

Sometimes 20 parcels from Evans & Owens had to be delivered at Kensington and Batheaston. The Globe, Newton, was the only public house tramwaymen were allowed in in uniform as it was a parcel office, and the crew sometimes made up dummy parcels to give them an excuse to go in!

In September 1910 the tramways were even more ambitious, becoming goods and travel agents, the following notice appearing in the timetable: 'Foreign Freight. The Company are now prepared to Collect or Receive Goods & Parcels, Motor Cars, Cycles, Pianos, Livestock etc. for conveyance to and from all parts of the world. Removals abroad at lowest rates'. 'Passages to any part of the Globe.' 'Licensed emigration agents.'

By 1931 the Head Parcels Office was now at 26, Dorchester Street, but parcels could also be received for both collection and delivery at 12, Newbridge Hill, Walcot tram depot, Kensington bus garage, the Glasshouse Café, the Globe Inn, 14 agencies in retail shops in the city and suburbs, and 50 similar agencies in retail shops or public houses in towns and villages throughout the area served by the company's buses. There were 12 different scales of charges, namely for the Town Area, the Suburban Area, and outlying districts including Bus Routes, sub-divided in each case as between delivery only and both collection and delivery, and also as between parcels containing glass, china, and fragile or bulky items, and all other parcels. The weight limits for charging purposes were up to 3, 7, 12, 20, 28, 36, 45, 56, 70, 84, 98, and 112 lbs, and 'each additional 28 lbs', with no maximum stated. This gave 144 different amounts, even excluding parcels over 112 lbs, which must have been a nightmare for conductors and agencies. The highest rate was 2s. 6d. for a fragile parcel of 112 lbs including collection from an outlying district, plus 9d. more for an extra 28 lbs.

The Wells Road accident, 3rd July, 1933. Cars No. 6 (*left*) and No. 18 (*right*) collided on single track and stopped in the loop. Stan Curtess is tying down the trolley boom of No. 18, while the dash of No. 6 is smashed back to the floor.   *Author's Collection*

Car 32 at the Guildhall on 19th July, 1909 decorated to advertise the Bath Pageant. The various signs in the windows advertise available excursions. *Author's Collection*

Car 6 in the depot yard, February 1923. This event to help the unemployed was organised by a sub-committee of the tramway's Recreation Committee. Two appearances of the car raised over £33. A similarly decorated charabanc toured parts of the city not covered by tram routes. *Author's Collection*

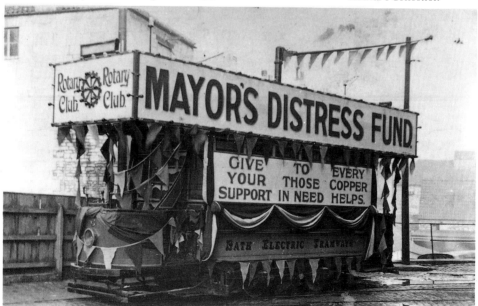

Chapter Seven
Accidents

The first accident occurred only a week after opening — on 9th January, 1904 when single-deck car No. 50 which was working from Devonshire Buildings to Bathford went partly out of control, struck a coal cart near the bottom of the Wells Road, continued on and struck another, killing a horse, and becoming derailed. The dash was bent and its headlight damaged. In consequence of No. 50 becoming disabled, McCarter was unable to open the Oldfield Park route on 11th January as he had intended.

On 19th April, 1904, a car ran away down Combe Park through some inexplicable cause, was derailed below the Weston Hotel, and collided with the wall of Locksbrook Cemetery. A less serious series of accidents occurred on 5th August when car after car came off the rails on the Nile Street/Upper Bristol Road curve. Four cars in succession were derailed about 10 pm and crowds of onlookers 'found the spectacle entertaining'.

The Weston Hotel was the scene of another derailment on 25th November, 1906, when car No. 33 turned over after destroying the garden walls at Ashley Terrace. The car ran out of control as the reversing handle was in the wrong position and the magnetic brakes would only operate if the starting handle was set for the direction in which the car was travelling. The injured motorman was taken to the Royal United Hospital in another car rather than in the waiting ambulance as this was thought more expeditious. The conductor suffered hardly any injuries which was surprising considering he was thrown from the upper deck. About 12 hours after the accident, the car was righted and was so little damaged that it was driven back to the depot under its own power. Five days later, to restore public confidence in the brakes, Hardy, the deputy manager, and Seckington, traffic superintendent, gave a demonstration to the press by safely going down the Wells Road with the trolley pole tied down. They showed that the handbrake was capable of holding a car on a steep hill as long as speed was reduced by the magnetic brakes.

On 19th April, 1916 two cars passed in the loop at the Weston Hotel. When the Weston car had gone 14 yds up Newbridge Hill, the driver found the wheels were slipping on wet tar and the brakes would not hold. The car ran back and the automatic points at the entrance to the loop put the runaway on the same road as the other car. The motorman of the stationary car, warned of its approach, released his brakes to reduce the impact. Both cars ran to the foot of the hill where they stopped.

Three months later on 17th July, an Oldfield Park car was rounding the bend from Herbert Road into Cynthia Road when the switch blew, and, the motorman not applying his handbrake quickly enough, the car ran back down a gradient of 1 in 11. At Livingstone Road loop the car was derailed and plunged into the front garden of a house.

On 29th May, 1918, No. 12 set off from the Crown Inn while the conductress was collecting a parcel from the Newbridge Hill office. She blew her whistle and the woman driver set back a few yards to meet her. The conductress then boarded the car and rang it off. By the Weston Hotel the car was out of control. It failed to take the points beyond the Weston Hotel, ran

Car 12 overturned below the Weston Hotel on 29th May, 1918. A convalescent soldier from the Bath War Hospital stands on the right with a stick. Inset is a picture of Miss Beatrice Walker, the driver. *Author's Collection*

Another view of car 12 overturned by the entrance to Locksbrook Cemetery on 29th May, 1918. The upper deck has partly broken away from the lower. *T.C. Leaman*

down the road, hit a boundary wall and overturned. Many of the passengers on the upper deck clung to seats and railings to prevent themselves from being ejected, but Councillor Olinthus Newman was thrown out and killed. More than half of the 22 passengers were convalescent Australian soldiers from the Bath War Hospital at Combe Park. A steam lorry belonging to the Bath Gas Co. re-railed the truck and body floor 4½ hours after the accident, the rest of the car being removed in BET motor lorries. In the early evening, the truck of the overturned car was hauled to the top of Combe Park and the car run down by the rolling stock superintendent R. Dodd, who found the magnetic brakes functioned properly. Some thought, though it was never proved, that this was another case where the starting handle was not set for the direction of travel, so rendering the magnetic brakes inoperative.

The last fatal accident occurred at 4.55 pm on Monday, 3rd July, 1933, when No. 6 ascending the Wells Road, slipped on tar just before Hayesfield Park on a gradient of 1 in 11.6 and skidded backwards down the Wells Road, the brake blocks being covered with tar and failing to grip. No. 6 collided with No. 18 damaging the end of both cars. Two passengers were fatally injured, one through jumping off the car, and 37 others (25 on No. 6 and 12 on No. 18) were less seriously injured. None of the four drivers and conductors received more than a few bruises. It was an extremely hot day, with a temperature of 85.4°F at 6 pm. Car No. 6 was baulked by a slow-moving steam lorry which was also travelling up the hill, so the motorman cut off power, and the car stopped at a point where a patch of tar, softened by the heat, had spread over the near-side rail. When power was applied again the car wheels slipped, and although the driver applied sand the car did not move forward the few inches it needed to reach it, and started to run backwards. After 356 yards it collided with stationary car No. 18 which had been following it. Both trams then travelled in reverse for another 150 yards before stopping. Neither car was derailed, and the trolleys did not leave the wire. The front platform of car No. 18 over-rode the rear one of No. 6, but the damage to both trams was limited to the platforms, staircases, and canopies. The driver of runaway No. 6 applied and re-applied his magnetic brake seven times and the handbrake three times, and their combined efforts restricted the speed of the collision to about 10 mph.

An official Ministry of Transport Inquiry was held into this accident, and in the whole history of British tramways there were only about a hundred MoT or Board of Trade published accident enquiries from 1883 to 1959. Evidence was heard from the four drivers and conductors involved; the driver of the tram which went up the hill five minutes previously; the City Engineer; his deputy; the tramways superintendent; the chief inspector; the depot charge-hand fitter; the tramways rail cleaner; and two passengers. Lt Col. E. Woodhouse of the MoT published his Report on 19th September, 1933, a document of 10 closely-typed foolscap pages. He said that the Tramway Company had an excellent record of freedom from serious accidents, despite severe gradients, and Car No. 6 was in a proper state of maintenance with no mechanical faults, and that its driver had a good record of 20 years of tramway service, 14 as a driver, but that he ought to have used his handbrake more and his magnetic brake less, when running backwards.

He said the main cause of the accident was that the road surface had been re-tarred so many times during previous years that soft tar had built up in places to one inch above the surface of the rails, and that in places he had poked a knife blade 1¼ in. down into the tar before meeting solid stone. He recommended that all this surplus tar should be scraped off, especially on hilly sections of route, and also that the tramcars should be modified so that the motorman could have direct control, either by electrical or mechanical means, of the sanding gear at the rear of the car as well as the front, so that sand could be put directly under the rear wheels instead of the conductor throwing it over the dashboard about 6 or 8 feet ahead of the wheels, when only some of it would actually land on the rails.

Car 50 derailed in Livingstone Road on 18th July, 1916. The accident occurred when the breaker switch blew as the tram rounded the corner from Herbert Road into Cynthia Road, the car running back out of control. Derailed, it ended in a garden. The car bears the BET monogram and a 'Guildhall' side destination board.

Mrs G. Norris Collection